RUNNING AWAY

A Memoir of Opportunity

JOHN McCREEDY

Dedication

I dedicate this book to Frank O'Mara,
one of the finest athletes and inspirational figures
Ireland has ever produced.

© John McCreedy, 2025.
The moral rights of the author have been asserted.
ISBN: 978-1-9192724-0-5

CONTENTS

Acknowledgements	4
Foreword	6
A Word from America	8
Preface	10
Beginnings	13
Mentor McKnight	23
'The Mary P'	33
A Dance with Bridget	43
"Hello, John, It's America Calling"	53
JR, Southfork and Choices	63
Silence Isn't Always Golden	73
"Hey, John, You Don't Know Me"	83
Leaving Loch Lao - Saying Goodbye	93
"Welcome to America, John!"	103
"Does Anyone Know Where Ireland Is?"	113
A Horse Between Two Mattresses	123
Partygate and Pizzagate 1980	133
Thanksgiving and Christmas with the Curriers	143
On the Road Again	151
A Snake in The Night	161
The Last Lap	171
Epilogue	180
Notes to the Text	182

Acknowledgements

My local athletics coach, Tony McKnight, friend, father figure, and general inspiration, helped make my youth indelibly memorable. Although he passed away far too young, Tony remains one of the most extraordinary and unforgettable characters to grace my life. What lay in store for me as a teenager would never have blossomed without him. Words could never adequately thank him, and I treasure his memory every day and miss him terribly.

"If ifs and buts were candy and nuts, it would be Christmas all year." (Dave Suenram, Hall of Fame Track Coach at Pittsburg State University.)

The above is the most memorable and appropriate of all the quotes I remember from my American coach, Dave Suenram. I have tried to follow his ethos and approach in my own life. I have carried his impartation and teaching since I first met him as a young athlete. Dave Suenram, who lived to the age of eighty, sadly passed away in 2015, which profoundly affected me, but his athletic achievements and impact in general remain legendary. I, along with many others privileged to compete for him, will never forget his contributions to Pittsburg State University (PSU) in Kansas and his importance to an entire generation of young sports students. I can only second what others have said about him – 'he was as outstanding a man as ever there was.'

They say the difference between a good friend and a best friend is that a good friend knows all your stories, but a best friend helps you write them. That's true of my good friend and former Pitt State teammate, Scott Currier. Thank you, Scott, and your wonderful family for some fantastic memories and lasting friendship. Even in this project, your support in offering valuable information and backing has been greatly appreciated. I am most grateful.

'Some man for one man' is how I would describe my dear friend, Roddy Gaynor. A success in athletics in Ireland both as a competitor and coach, as well as his exploits at Pittsburg State, Roddy was priceless to me as a friend and colleague during my time in America, for which I can never thank him enough.

But Roddy has proved more than a talented athlete and college buddy. He is a first-class individual and the best role model for many aspiring young sports people in Ireland and even further afield.

Rick Webb is the Chief Executive Officer of Watco, a hugely successful rail transportation service provider based in Pittsburg. As much as anyone, he has embraced opportunities to improve life for the city's people and the surrounding area through his highly commendable support for PSU and the many local schools and community organisations. I remain in awe of my former teammate Rick's outstanding achievements and commitment to Pittsburg State University and sincerely appreciate his agreeing to read this book before publication.

When I thought all the hidden helpers had gone, along came my Editor, Patrick McGarry. Although we met later in life, it's as though we have been friends for many years. Without question, this book would not have reached publication without Patrick's many painstaking hours of editing and beneficial advice. I feel highly blessed and privileged to know Patrick and to have such a distinguished writer and author critique and improve this work. Thank you, Patrick, for your friendship, professionalism, and fantastic sense of humour.

Gee Finlay of Belfast Central Library has my deepest appreciation for his meticulous attention in recovering essential newspaper clippings from the archive.

And a big 'Thank You' also to the wonderful staff at The Linen Hall Library in Belfast for all their kind assistance and quiet forbearance. Working at The Library countless times over many months, during 2024/25 on this manuscript with my dedicated editor, Patrick, was a joy and a privilege. They have my enduring gratitude.

Finally, it would be remiss of me, not to mention all my family who sacrificed so much to facilitate my athletics career. I was blessed with good parents, grandparents and peerless siblings. Thank you, guys! Your love and encouragement always brought out the best in me.

Foreword

'Running Away,' by John McCreedy, a talented writer and runner from Co Down, is a book that succeeds on many levels. It is enjoyable, educational, witty, wise, and a real page-turner. It was a joy to read and is a true work of literature. It will be a wonderful addition to the creative canon and the shelves of our bookstores and libraries across the province and beyond. In an era with a clear dearth of great book titles, John's work is already a winner: memorable, enriched by multiple meanings, engaging and immediate. Without giving anything away, reading his oeuvre is an absolute pleasure - no spoilers!

The world of competitive sports is his canvas; he knows it inside and out. I'm convinced his book will continue to be an excellent source of encouragement and delight, especially for young people and those with ambitions to succeed in the highly competitive world of sport, particularly in the elite arena of the track.

What is unique about John's story is that, having won a prestigious athletic scholarship to a university in the Midwest of America in the Eighties, he was blessed, with the facilities and support he needed during his stay in Kansas. Rarely does one see or come across a testament to what that experience looked like in reverse, as it were, when his time in America ended. It was always a struggle for him to gather the funds he needed before leaving Ireland.

Today, support services are available for young hopefuls to concentrate more on their goals rather than exhaustive searches for income to support them.

The struggles in John's day were very real and, palpable.

The young athlete was fortunate in another way, though. And a crucial one. During his stay in the States, he met coaches, trainers, mentors, and new friends who provided unexpected and unwavering support, understanding, and kindness, all of which contributed to keeping him on the right track. It was a lifeline to a young man far from home, at times lonely, yet never forlorn, for he was something of a novelty to his Kansas hosts. A young Irishman fleeing, as they saw it, his homeland then 'in flames,' but who ultimately put his faith in his destiny. They all wanted to know his story. Now they can. Every student-athlete going on a scholarship to America must read this book.

'Running Away' is a lyrical and easy read, and I wish John every success with this fascinating memoir. I really enjoyed it, and I hope you will, too.

Lady Mary Peters
Belfast, September 2024

A Word from America

I had the distinct pleasure of meeting John McCreedy when he was an emerging track athlete from Ireland. He relocated to my small hometown in Kansas to compete as a Pittsburg State Gorilla, and I was impressed by his unique perspective on life and the challenges it presents. John possesses an extraordinary ability to connect with people from all walks of life, forging friendships that endure despite the everyday obstacles we all face.

In his compelling book, "Running Away," John shares the inspiring journey of a young man who fully commits to his dream of becoming a world-class track athlete. This young man moves to a different country without a safety net, experiences initial success, but ultimately encounters the harsh realities of temporary setbacks and failures. John masterfully recounts his struggles to achieve his dream, navigating numerous obstacles, some stemming from the carelessness of those he trusted, and ultimately triumphing against the odds.

John has a remarkable talent for crafting a story that captivates and resonates with readers—a narrative that is not only entertaining but also profoundly relatable.

I strongly encourage you to dive into "Running Away." This recommendation comes not just because I am proud to call John my friend, but because his story reminds us of the necessary importance of nurturing and valuing the relationships that help us persevere through life's challenges.

Rick Webb, Pitt State, 2024

Preface

Hidden Helpers

I started this book during the dreaded Lockdown when, surprise, surprise, my athletic adventures came running back to me like a lost lover. It was as if they'd lain dormant for almost 40 years. How could this have been?

With time to think and reflect, I suddenly realised how privileged this part of my life in the 1980's was. While writing this personal account, I've recalled escaping, as a teenager, some of the Northern Ireland Troubles while reluctantly revealing a few of the laughable antics I got up to at an American University – Pittsburg State (with a G) in Kansas. Since then, I've discovered that life is the most fantastic race we will ever run. It is unpredictable, with highs and lows, joy and pain, with an endpoint somewhere.

However, my greatest motivation to complete and publish this book wasn't just to relate a small part of my athletic adventures and how this influenced my life's journey. The numerous hidden helpers I encountered along the way became the real inspiration. They were instrumental in helping me achieve many dreams I couldn't have realised on my own. From athletics coaches and enthusiasts to church workers to people in business, to dear friends and to others who displayed extraordinary acts of kindness. I look back in amazement at the mentorship and support I received.

The more I recalled, reminisced and wrote, the more I realised I could not have achieved a quarter of what I experienced without these heroes. So, this book is as much about them as it is about me. It's a massive shout-out to those people who sacrificed on my behalf.

I am convinced that no one has attained their goals without what I would describe as a hidden helper. We all need someone to raise us higher than we can be – a heaven-sent individual. Helpers like these are everywhere, but we can't always see them. They seek no recognition. Fame and glory are not part of their makeup. These unselfish, generous, and extraordinary people are happy to "stand back" and watch others achieve their lifetime goals. They possess that most excellent quality of 'thinking of others before themselves.'

Of course, we don't always appreciate such people assigned to assist us in reaching our destinies, but we are doomed to stumble and fail without them.

The American writer C.J. Heck wrote: "We are all products of our environment; every person we meet, every new experience or adventure, every book we read touches and changes us, making us the unique beings we are."

Without the commitment of those early volunteers, mentors, helpers, and family, the fantastic opportunity I received through the sport of athletics wouldn't have happened. Even those waiting to 'push me forward' on the other side of the Atlantic - when I arrived in America like a fish out of water - played a vital part in making my dreams come true. So, I gladly and gratefully dedicate this book to them and place a gold medal around their necks.

Mum and the twins.

John with twin James and Jillian.

Chapter One – Beginnings

I was born in Bangor, Co Down. Although situated just down the coast from Belfast, our seaside town seemed a world away from the daily death and destruction experienced at that time in the nearby capital city of Northern Ireland.

Growing up in Bangor, a mainly Protestant coastal town, was a privilege many Bangorians like me didn't perhaps fully appreciate. Aside from the bombs, bullets, paramilitary activity, and premature deaths associated with 'The Troubles,' life remained more comfortable and secure for us than in other places in the province. While the threat of violence was always there, of course – even visiting our beautiful town one tragic day – it must be said we were mainly on the periphery.

Post-World War II, waves of day trippers travelled to Bangor from all over Ireland and Scotland. It was the largest seaside resort on the island, famous for 'The Bangor Boat' and its long association with St Columbanus and many other well-known missionaries and evangelists. Known as 'The New Jerusalem' and 'The Valley of Angels,' Bangor was once one of early Medieval Ireland's foremost monastic centres of study and learning.

RUNNING AWAY

During my youth, Bangor was a very popular destination. Families continued to flock to the seaside and Barry's Amusement Arcade in droves. It opened decades before, in 1927, on the site of the Grand Hotel, when the latest fairground amusements and dodgems arrived, including the famous ghost train. I still remember Mrs. Delino running about with her massive bunch of keys (which had opened various slot machines). How she correctly placed each one was a complete mystery. Nothing bettered the laughing policeman, though. It was vintage!

Unlike today, at the beginning of the 1970s, there was no expensive marina, boarded-up shops, or graffiti-daubed buildings on the seafront— just a stony beach with slippery seaweed, empty cider bottles, and ruined sandcastles. We might describe it as progress in reverse! We wore ridiculous-looking flares and platform shoes, rode chopper bikes, and played on space hoppers. In those halcyon days, you could sleep on the beach and still make it home without incident the next day, at least until we tried explaining ourselves to our parents.

Bangor's youth met safely on the sea wall, demolishing fish and chips from iconic eateries like Paul's and Ken's, followed by ice cream at an overabundance of competing outlets. Like many other children in Bangor, I'd learned to swim at Pickie Pool – arguably one of the coldest outdoor pools in the world. Pickie opened decades before, in 1931, and despite its icy water, it quickly became known as the "go-to place for swimmers and divers" for over 50 years.

It wasn't fun seeing numerous kids shiver to the top of the diving board, only to drop into an icebox.

My friends would suggest, "Let's all go to Pickie." "What a not-so-nice idea," I thought to myself.

Once there, dropping off that board made my stomach churn. If you didn't jump, you were labelled a chicken! So, we were going into that 'icebox' whether we liked it or not. When the big rush was finally over, I remember we scampered to the sea behind the legendary pool in search of any natural heat. With Belfast Lough's shores often proving warmer than the local swimming pool, I always felt there should have been a warning sign at Pickie saying, 'Danger. Don't go in!'

Since then, winter and cold-water swimming has become more fashionable, of course. We didn't have long, nomadic, recycled sherpa-lined black swimming robes to wrap around us. Years ago, seeing these slow-moving, middle-aged, overweight gothic-like creatures, some in their chunky dunkers, tip-toeing into the water would have cleared the beach and made even the sharks in 'Jaws' scatter. Roy Scheider would have loved them!

I never won a swimming race at Pickie nor a diving contest, only a singing competition with a rendition of Edelweiss – my first and last attempt at a musical career. An old photograph showing me dressed like I was in The Sound of Music remains mortifying, especially as my mother still hands it out. That photo included my twin brother James and another set of Bangor twins – the McCully's. There was no rivalry between us boys, yet our mothers insisted on dressing us the same, something we lads never quite got. We weren't identical; it must have been a twin thing! Fast-forward a half-century, the Pickie our generation knew has been transformed into an imposing Fun Park showcasing an 18-hole mini-golf course, giant pedal swans, a Pickie Puffer train, a children's play area, an electric car track, and splash pads.

What's not to like about that?

But, in the Sixties and Seventies, Pickie was just a pool, a place to let off steam and forget the dangers of 'The Troubles.' Indeed, the name Pickie became virtually synonymous with Bangor itself. Like the choppy waves surrounding Pickie, domestic life had proved challenging in those formative years for James, me, and our adorable baby sister, Jillian. She was born seven years after us and was the cutest toddler on the block. Everyone loved cute little Jillian. We would flick her nose and ears and bounce her up and down, then get a telling-off from Mum, who said we were far too rough with her. James and I only envied and resented my sister once, when Mum took her to Australia at age ten, leaving us lads behind with our loveable but laidback father.

He was no match for my mother in the kitchen. He was a good dad, but no Jamie Oliver or Gordon Ramsay. When I commented one night that the stew wasn't like Mum's and was too runny, my dad snapped, "Sup it up, you ungrateful little boy, or I'll send you to Africa." So, I continued to 'slurp' it up and thanked God for every mouthful, curious about what

everyone was having, not in Africa, but 10,000 miles away in Adelaide, South Australia. That said, it wasn't only the stew's poor quality that made me curious about my dad in those days. Enjoying a cigarette, he would often stand in the backyard of our house and stare into the sky as if looking for inspiration or damage on the roof. He regularly did it, but I can never recall any repairs being done by him or anyone else.
"What do you think Dad's doing, staring up into the sky like that?" I would ask my brother James.

"Not sure; maybe he's talking to God", he replied.
"That, or waiting on Mum's plane returning, and he's not the only one," I suggested.

I dreamed of Mum's Shepherd's Pie, Steak and Carrot with mash, and Sunday Roast with chicken or roast beef.

Our dad was out a lot in those days, but not for business. It was the 'Swinging Sixties' when the lad's culture reigned supreme. Beatlemania, Radio Caroline, Mods and Rockers, parallels, and flared trousers were the order of the day. Many men would skilfully slip out of the house each night as if they needed cigarettes or were on an undercover mission to bring back potato crisps for their kids. Strangely, they always found the cigarettes, but the crisps never arrived, and neither did the lads.

In those developmental years, I clung to massive sporting dreams. It gave me hope. Despite the tensions caused by The Troubles involving our two largest communities, I longed to be a sports star, but which sport? A 'Jack of all trades,' I was handy at most ball games apart from rugby and cricket from an early age. Looking back, I had no interest in cricket; it was much too pedestrian, while rugby was far too rough on my skinny, lean frame. The closest I would get to the Six Nations would be selling match-day programmes, watching from the stands, or observing the live game on TV in a chic Dublin hotel.

There could never be a place in the Irish rugby team for someone as slight as me, not even on the wing. Yet for some reason, the school rugby coach insisted I play it. I remember avoiding him after getting mangled by a massive-looking prop forward from Regent House Grammar, in Newtownards (Co. Down), with an eye on the School's Cup final, a youngster who couldn't have been the same age as me. A powerhouse, he was taught to extinguish everything in his path and stuck to the plan. I couldn't walk for several weeks after getting bundled into the railings.

Job done!

Although keen on various racket sports, like many young boys my age, I was determined to become a professional footballer one day. Every Sunday morning, I would chase after my dad through Bangor's Ward Park to get the Sunday papers, which included a copy of the famous 'Billy's Boots.' This trendy British comic strip began in 1961, the same year my twin and I were born and lasted until 1990 when 'Roy of the Rovers' replaced it. As we passed the tennis courts on one side and the river on the other, headed for Bloomfield Stores, a well-known shop in the town, I wasn't interested in candy or crisps, only in getting my hands on a copy of 'Billy's Boots.' In terms of sporting popularity, it was the Harry Potter of my generation.

Every aspiring young footballer read 'Billy's Boots.' I would plead excitedly, "Dad, would you buy me 'Billy's Boots', please, please, pretty please, Dad?" I recall torturing my poor father the whole way there until he gave in, saying: "If it's in, son."

Too often, however, 'Billy's Boots' wasn't in, which left me feeling deflated, but when it did appear, I was obsessed for the rest of the day, reading about Billy's incredible exploits with a ball. Speaking of Ward Park, back in the day, it was famous for international bowlers, the bandstand, and underage drinking; a place where youthful misdemeanour was lavish. It boasted an immaculate playing surface beside the War Memorial, which we called 'Wembley.' Often used for soccer games, even though it was forbidden, we would cover with dark mud the sign saying, "No Football Allowed", and play until the park-keeper arrived. Then, when he turned up unexpectedly, we would run for our lives regardless of who was winning. One night, we even managed to nearly ruin the prestigious and famous Bangor Bowling Green opposite the War Memorial with a five-a-side game. Creating, at the same time, a front-page headline in a local paper - "Thugs destroy Bangor Bowling Green."

"Who would do such an outrageous thing?" commented Mum, while reading the editorial exclusive in the local paper. I kicked my brother under the table, winked at him, and responded, "Disgraceful behaviour;

these people should be ashamed of themselves!"

Much of my childhood memories involve the self-same Ward Park. We lived in a terraced house directly opposite the park. It was so central that we didn't appreciate how close everything was. The shops and local church were just around the corner, we attended Bangor Central Primary School, which was also on our doorstep, and the local library and Bangor Hospital were within yards of our home.

In those carefree, bygone days, we were never out of Ward Park. From playing crazy golf in the putting ground (also outlawed) to a case of experiencing mistaken identity after being chased through the park by an angry father, convinced I was seeing his sought-after daughter, to having my first-ever kiss with another girl behind a shed, ruined when my brother arrived and announced: "John, your tea is ready."

When it came to girls and food, it was often James' timing that was atrocious! I was always at the dinner table at 5 p.m. sharp, but there would be no sign of James. Mum would go to the edge of the park at 'the bank' and, without needing a loud hailer, she would shout, "Jaaaaaaaaaaaames, your dinner is ready." Sometimes, he could hear her at Ballyholme. It sounded like an Air Raid siren during The War. What the neighbours used to think, God only knows!

The list of tomfoolery at Ward Park is endless, like the legendary penalty competitions we had beside the bowling green, using two trees as posts, oblivious that the ball consistently careered towards the cars opposite us on Park Drive – coincidentally, the name of a very famous brand of cigarettes at that time. Any accident on Park Drive was usually, if not always, the result of one of our penalty kicks. We were known as the boys from Castle Street. We had a half-decent football team and played in a Bangor league without administration or officials. We played teams from Clandeboye, Kilcooley, Crawfordsburn, Towerview, Bryansburn and Bloomfield. Anything went in that league. There was no such thing as VAR. If a goal was in doubt, those who shouted the loudest usually got their way. The team was run by two slightly older guys, Roy Lyle and David Delaney. We looked up to them, not because they were remarkable. They were just older. We were all shocked when they fell out and agreed to fight each other one morning at dawn.

The big bout was to take place at the playing fields opposite Gransha Road, and word quickly spread. Most of my friends couldn't sleep due to excitement. I was sad that they were planning to beat the daylights out of each other. I liked both of them. It was our version of Ali versus Frazier or Frampton versus Martinez. We all rose early that morning and waited for the two boxers to arrive, but neither Lyle nor Delaney weighed in for the Big Bangor Rumble in the Jungle. We never did find out why, but I suspect it was for one of three reasons. They were having us on, they slept in, or both were afraid. Whichever, our role models had, it seemed feet of clay, after all.

"If you could remember your homework like you can name every player in the First Division, you would be top of the class," my mother often said sarcastically. She was right. When it came to football, I had a photographic memory.

Mum had her hands full in those days and always seemed a little on edge. With three children, a full-time job, and running a dance school, she didn't have much time for herself. God bless her. She was more concerned with giving us all a good upbringing. Once, when I was about twelve, I remember Mum took me to the old Woolworths or Wellworths store on Bangor's Main Street - not sure which one as they were beside each other then. As we approached the door, she held it open for a customer who passed by without acknowledging her.

Wrong move!

Mum was a stickler for good manners and had drummed 'please' and 'thank you' into her three children from birth. "Manners maketh the man!" Mum consistently told us. When the customer failed to acknowledge her, without warning and to my absolute horror, she shouted at the top of her voice, "THANK YOU!". It was so loud her voice could be heard in High Street, let alone Main Street. So, I did what most teenagers would have done in such a situation. I scattered, disowning my mother.

When she eventually caught up with me, livid and red-faced, I asked: "Was there any need for that, mum?" "There was every need. He is a most ignorant man," she swiftly replied. Mum always told it like it was. On another occasion, she bumped into what she described as "a chancer" at the Bangor Market on Wednesday. Waiting in a long queue for fish,

RUNNING AWAY

Mum was just about to be served when a rude woman cut-in, in front of her. After a brief contretemps, the lady declared: "I'm from Ballyholme, you know!"

"Good for you, I'm from Bangor - and Next!" replied my mother. Catfight, over.

She was always right about my love for football, however. The Old English First Division (now Premier League) became my obsession. I could name the entire Everton squad – my boyhood team - and imagined many times running out to star for the *Super Toffees* at the famous Goodison Park stadium in Liverpool. I carried copious cards with pictures of every player, particularly the No. 10, Duncan MacKenzie, who was my favourite. I loved how he rolled his socks down to his ankles, and his skill was off the chart! He was from that extraordinary generation of silky players like George Best, Stan Bowles, Tony Currie, Frank Worthington and Rodney Marsh. Mackenzie had me imagining scoring the winning goal in the Merseyside Derby (against Liverpool!) a thousand times over – even with my less reliable left foot.

While we're on Everton versus Liverpool, I have never quite got over what happened in the 1977 FA Cup semi-final. With the score locked at 2-2, Northern Ireland international Bryan Hamilton chested in a worthy goal to make it 3-2 to the Toffees in the match's dying minutes. I played table tennis at a friend's house that afternoon when Hamilton appeared to give Everton a thrilling victory. Like a shot, I bolted out of his garage door and sprinted down the street with my arms aloft, only to be told that the referee, Clive Thomas, had ruled out the goal. At various points afterwards, Thomas implied that the goal was disallowed due to handball, even though Hamilton diverted the ball past the Liverpool goalkeeper, Ray Clemence, with his hip.

Of course, as I've said, there was no VAR back then, just a ref who got it wrong–very wrong! Everton lost the replay and was out of the cup. Years later, Thomas admitted that he'd made a mistake, which, although generous, was a case of too little, too late! In my humble opinion, it is still the worst decision ever made at a football match, yes, worse than Thierry Henry's handball for France against Ireland in 2009, which eliminated the Irish from the 2010 World Cup and even worse than the infamous Hand of God moment when the late, great Diego Maradona denied England from progressing in the 1986 World Cup. Those were genuine, blatant, unforgivable handballs, which somehow were allowed to stand, but not Bryan Hamilton's eccentric effort. It was a magnificent goal, unjustifiably cancelled, almost spoiling my youth. I still haven't got over it!

In those days, my local Presbyterian church taught us about the Holy Trinity of Father, Son, and Holy Ghost. I sang in the choir. However, when it came to the Trinity, I seemed more interested in the legendary Everton version of Ball, Harvey, and Kendall at that stage. Like Dixie Dean before them, Howard Kendall, Alan Ball, and Colin Harvey attained football immortality at Goodison Park, and these were my sporting idols back then.

A favourite memory of mine was when Alan Ball announced to his dad one evening that he would play in white boots for the first time on a Saturday. The story goes that his father, who was reading the newspaper, quickly put it down, looked over his glasses, and commented, "By golly, you better be good, son!" I bought a similar pair of white boots, but they didn't help me make the grade. I was no Alan Ball. Ultimately, divine providence-or, more probably, lack of ability-ensured that a professional football career at home or 'across the water' wasn't in the stars for me. But it was far from the end of my sporting destiny. An unexpected new challenge and sport was about to consume me, changing my entire direction. From there on, I would be 'running away 'in more ways than one.

Tony McKnight.

Chapter Two - Mentor McKnight

I had never imagined losing interest in soccer, but it happened when self-glorification presented itself. Chosen to represent my school at a cross-country running event, I didn't want to participate until I heard that my brother had won the week before. Sibling rivalry is a magnificent form of motivation! It can go back to childhood in the pram when we fought for the best apple. I usually won and handed James the inferior one, which wasn't strictly brotherly love!

"You were always the mischievous one," said Mum once we'd grown up. Nevertheless, that day at Ballymacormick, near Groomsport, I'd turned up in white plimsolls - remember the famous gutties? I soon ignored the bog-like conditions and romped to victory in my first-ever race without training!

From there on, I was hooked and didn't stop running, while James never ran another step, which was a shame. I'm convinced he could easily have been a top-class runner and miles better than me if he'd wanted. My twin was considerably taller, had a better stride length and possessed a tremendous engine. Ultimately, he was the only rival in Northern Ireland I feared, yet he showed no interest in athletics, which suited me down to the ground. I could win all by myself!

RUNNING AWAY

Soon, training and running gripped me. Eventually, I invested in proper running shoes and spikes and discovered something quite satisfying. Unlike soccer, where the outcome depends on the team's performance, everything I did was down to me, and I enjoyed that. The individualism in athletics hooked me; the opportunity to shine alone rather than as part of a team. It's called ego!

I would no longer have to sit freezing on the sidelines as a substitute for my local BB football team, and I would be more in control of my future. Furthermore, I learned I could run like the wind, though not in the sprinting manner of Usain Bolt. Stamina, rather than sprinting ability, was my main strength. I was known as a 'middle to long-distance journeyman,' enjoying, in those days, the beautiful parklands and coastal courses close to my home daily. I'd read about British distance runner Dave Bedford, who famously trained in hob-nail boots. Then, he would put his spikes on and fly on race day. I tried the same formula wearing the boots running one day, but it was my first and last attempt. Hobbling back home, I almost ended my athletics career before it had even begun!

Trainers tied and ready to go, I was never more content than gliding over the muddy grass at Bangor's Ward and Castle Parks twice daily, instantly discovering how running took me to another realm. Whether my training sessions were on track, on the sandy beach at Ballyholme or jogging through the beautiful rural area at Crawfordsburn Country Park, a few miles from our house, spiritual release and life ambition collided the same day. Fleet of foot, running became not just a sport but a profoundly transcendental experience I never felt playing soccer. Suddenly, I could see beauty in every creature and part of creation. I couldn't wait to pull on my vest and shorts and 'go for a run.' The only negative thing about the training was, the many dogs chasing after my skinny, weather-beaten legs. One large Alsatian at the Valentine Playing Fields was hell-bent on biting me every time he saw me.

I was scared stiff of that dog, detested him, and he hated me. It was like a cat-and-mouse game between us whenever I emerged from the woods. On days when the dog wasn't there, I would breathe a sigh of relief, but on other days, I fled for my life. Even though I would later become a 'dog lover', I remember hearing how that dog had died a few years later, and it brought me no sense of remorse. Once past this beast, I adored the sunlight shining through the trees in summer, while the mist from my breath on cold winter mornings reminded me that I was alive and well. I believed I had been created to run in life, even though I didn't understand why at that stage of my life's journey. I had taken to running like a duck to water!

The famous athlete and Scottish missionary Eric Liddell of 'Chariots of Fire' fame once said, "I believed God made me for a purpose, but He also made me fast. And when I run, I can feel his pleasure." That's how I felt, as well.

Notwithstanding, it would be many years before I could link the joy of running with physical and spiritual benefits. And so, despite continuing to play soccer until well into my teens, by age 15, my athletics career was king! Football had been well and truly eclipsed. Everything revolved around training and racing. Even mealtimes had to be scheduled to accommodate the daily training programme. Did I feel guilty about this, given I had a twin brother and younger sister at home?

Yes, I did, but I was highly driven and determined to be my best. What should have caused no end of friction and jealousy between my brother and sister remarkably didn't. James and Jillian were always firmly behind me and wanted me to succeed. If ever anyone was blessed with wonderful siblings, it was me. Eventually, James was too busy with music gigs around the country in a successful pop band named 'Dark Tower' and later as lead guitarist with the emerging 'Motion Pictures' to participate in sport. At the same time, Jillian had found puppy love and was never home. In due course, my brother's love and passion for music took him in a different direction. James was known as the 'Jimi Hendrix' of Bangor.

In the late 1970's, at a 'Dark Tower' concert in our hometown of Bangor, I recall hundreds of young people turning up to hear him and the band. The community hall was so filled with smoke and the music so loud that it became difficult to find anyone, or even to hear yourself think. Our Nanda had come to support James and was acting strangely, walking about, shouting up into the air like someone demented. "Ardglass herrings, two for a pound," he kept repeating. Of course, I thought he'd lost the plot. These were a tasty delicacy exclusively found in the coastal village and fishing port of Ardglass, Co Down. Concerned for him, I rightly asked Nanda why he behaved like a market seller at a rock concert until he replied, "No one can see me or hear me, so it doesn't matter what you say here." And on he went.

I couldn't argue. Nanda always had a wry sense of humour.

At a much larger event a few years later, I managed the band that evening when James and his renamed group Motion Pictures played a support act for the recognised British new wave band Kajagoogoo at the recently opened Maysfield Leisure Centre on Belfast's Waterfront. What did I know about pop band management? I was an aspiring athlete! But unusual opportunities arrive when your brother is the lead guitarist in a thriving local band. It was a big night for James and his fellow band members, and they didn't disappoint. After the group had given a good account of themselves, Kajagoogoo hit the stage to a packed hall. But not before the lead singer, Limahl, proved not "too shy" to provide me with a peck on the cheek, signing off with: "See you, sweetie," then sprinting onto the stage to his delighted fans. Thousands of girls would have died for such a moment!

Running, however, not music, was by then my focus. After some initial success, my athletics career took off at my local athletics club, North Down AC, under the guidance of dedicated and experienced coach Billy Brannigan. Advanced by another Northern Ireland coaching stalwart, Artie O'Neill, I was in the best hands, and it wasn't long before I flourished even more on the track thanks to someone who eventually became my long-term coach, mentor and friend – a charismatic and colourful character called Tony McKnight. I liked and respected Billy Brannigan, a terrific road runner and a gentleman. However, having resisted the offer to join Willowfield Harriers, a well-known distance running club at the time, I parted company with Billy. I plumped for the up-and-coming Belfast-based athletics stable Annadale Striders, where McKnight was the head coach.

Annadale was one of Ireland's most exciting athletic clubs at the time, so who wouldn't have been chuffed to get the opportunity to join them? The club was formed in 1973 when a small group gathered in Neil Morton's home to discuss setting up a new athletics club. The leading men were Morton and Tony McKnight. The club has enjoyed phenomenal success since, producing local athletics legends like Martin Girvan, Colin Boreham, John Doherty, John McLaughlin, Laurie Spence, Paul Lawther, Ernie Cunningham, Gary Lough, Richard Bleakley and Steve Martin, who all represented Great Britain. Philip Snoddy represented Ireland in the European Championships, and the Great Britain juniors include Paul Lawther, Steve McArthur, Mike Atkinson, Carson Porteous, John Reynolds, David Wilson, and Brian Treacy. At the same time, eighty-three Annadale juniors represented Northern Ireland, myself included.

Those were vintage days for me, training with great athletes and friends such as David Kilpatrick, David Leckey, Paul Lawther, Michael Lawther, Michael McKnight (Tony's son), Paul Younger, and Davy Smith, to name but a few. Some of these athletes were older, and some were better than me, pushing me to a higher standard. In days full of promise, the world was at my feet.

I can still recall how Tony, dubbed 'Mr Annadale Striders,' visited my mother at our Bangor home one night to try to sign me for Annadale. In his unique style, he left an unforgettable impression. My mother asked Tony: "Why is my son running so well?" Initially, I became embarrassed by the question until McKnight responded with a scientific explanation about how a bumblebee is so prominent in the body that it shouldn't be able to fly. "The bumblebee doesn't know it can't fly, so it buzzes everywhere. Your son is like the bumblebee. Ignorant of the times he's recording, he keeps getting quicker, and that's how I aim to keep it."

Mum loved it, and the rest was history. From that point, I was, in the words of the great Muhammad Ali, "floating like a butterfly and stinging like a bee." But McKnight became more than my athletic advisor, a dedicated and determined coach and engineer by profession; he became a significant mentor in my young and promising career, one of those first hidden helpers who impacted my youth. Like an additional family member, McKnight soon became the go-to person who helped with my sports career, specific work projects and general life advice. He was dedicated to his task and particularly protective of his group of young athletic stars in the making. I viewed him as a father figure. He certainly watched over me like one.

In the days before mobiles, Tony could find you anywhere. He would call me every night from his landline in Monkstown about my diet and training runs, but he wasn't all work and no play. He knew how to have fun, too.

Ultimately, we all grew to love and respect Tony. At the time, I had no idea how crucial he would become in my life back then. Unlike some fellow athletes, I wasn't doing well at school. All I could think about was sport. Over time, however, mentor McKnight not only kept tabs on my running stats but also invested significant time in my academic development by forcing me to do my homework, which, before meeting him, had always played second fiddle to my ambitions. McKnight's influence was crucial as he encouraged me to try and become the best I could be, not just at sports. I had no silver spoon to rely on, only hard graft and self-belief. In this respect, McKnight relentlessly got me to where I needed to be. Even my mother became exasperated at the numerous daily phone calls I received from him, always around teatime. We could put the kettle on for him!

"John, it's that man, Tony, again," Mum would shout up the stairs in a tone of resignation, if not exasperation.

"Okay, I'm coming now, Mum."

"Why does he always call as we are about to sit down for dinner?" Mum would say right over the phone so Tony could hear her.

It made no difference. McKnight would call again the next night at the same time, just as we were about to have our tea!

"All that man thinks about is athletics; has he no life?" Mum would often say. But athletics was his life. He lived and breathed every race and every training session.

He also cared immensely about his young athletes and imparted more than his sports knowledge. For example, Mum couldn't deny the difference this 'obsessive phone caller' was making in her son's school and sporting life. I had always been remarkably disciplined when it came to training, but suddenly, going to school and learning something was fun, not just playing football and carrying on! My mum was impressed by the change. I became what they call a 'late developer,' but better late than never. I had also become much more than one of Tony's athletes. I was a project, a goal, and a cause to my mentor, who relentlessly ensured I achieved my potential. It sounds OTT, but McKnight visited a local nightclub one night and hauled an ill-disciplined friend and me out of there before taking us home.

Today, we would call that 'obsessive concern for our welfare!' Tony saw it as 'duty.' "If you want to make the grade, John, and be the best, you can't go around burning the candle at both ends, and you shouldn't be keeping company with him," he growled, a reference to my partner in crime, a guy everyone knew as "Wee Jeff."

I knew McKnight was spot on regarding dedication to my sport, yet I couldn't help feeling incredibly sorry for my likeable wayward pal. He'd been degraded enough after his fake tan melted on his face while dancing with a girl that night, having waited two hours to approach her. Holding a pint bottle of milk (no one knew why) and dressed in a blue and yellow-striped t-shirt that merely exposed his skinny arms, he looked like Link Peterson (Stanley Tucci) in Shall We Dance.

"Don't you know you must 'wash your hands"!!! He was told.

Tony was wary of "Wee Jeff," believing him a bad influence on his more serious athletes, and he constantly warned me to stay away from him, but I adored him. My mother quickly arrived at the same conclusion as Tony, however. While staying at our house one Saturday, Jeff staggered down the stairs in the middle of the night and found a chicken slow-cooking for the Sunday roast the following day. Having just had a 'skinful', he was starving, leaving only the bones. The next day, the screams of my mother downstairs were louder than the traditional church bells or Salvation Army band that awakened the entire neighbourhood every Sunday morning outside. When "Wee Jeff" couldn't deny that he was the culprit who had scoffed our Sunday lunch, he was escorted from the house quicker than you could say 'Jack Robinson.'

Affectionately known as "Terrible Tony" due to his customary challenging of the rules laid down by the NIAAA (Northern Ireland Amateur Athletics Association), McKnight was particularly outspoken and a firm disciplinarian. He took no prisoners on and off the track. "I'll kick your butts", he would shout at my teammates and me if we dared to pass the lap mark at the newly built Mary Peters Track, a second slower than supposed to. Once, when a little boy shouted from the sidelines, 'Mummy, come and see the joggers,' McKnight snarled back at him, "Son, they're runners, not joggers."

Only Tony took his athletics that seriously!

Described as a wee man who did not suffer fools gladly, he called a spade a spade, which didn't endear him to everyone. But Tony was much loved by others, especially his athletes, who worshipped him, none more than me. He loved imitating another legendary Northern Ireland athletics enthusiast, Norman Bissett. Big Norman was "the salt of the earth," but he habitually criticised the local athletics authorities. Norman would describe some of the decision-making as "Fippin' ridiculous." There was no L in his Flippin'. It was just fippin'. It became a trademark saying everyone loved so much that when our batch of budding athletes came past McKnight's stopwatch slower than he expected, McKnight would gulder, "Fippin' ridiculous guys, get a move on."

But one more thing... McKnight had another reason for insisting on fast athletes and times; he always seemed in a hurry to get home and catch the weekly episode of Columbo, his favourite TV show. Oddly enough, Tony bore an uncanny resemblance to the unkempt lieutenant. Small in stature, he was always searching for a pen in his coat pockets, was a messy dresser, had jet-black hair, and was full of tricks. Like a man expecting a large cheque in the post, he would rub his hands together – even on a hot summer night at the track in mid-July when it wasn't cold - leaving most of his young prodigies scratching their heads.

"Why does he do that? " my colleagues and I would ask before setting off on another torturous lap of training under his supervision. When Tony turned up one night at the track wearing a tan-coloured raincoat, we all half expected him to produce a Basset Hound dog and sing 'Nick knack, paddy whack, Give the dog a bone.'

The adorable Basset Hound without a known name had leapt into collective hearts and minds in Colombo in 1972. The dozy beast, later known as 'Dog, ' made his screen debut in Columbo's season 2 opener, 'Etude in Black.' It was a love affair between man, dog, and viewer for over 40 years as Columbo became arguably the most incredible detective show ever. And we wondered why Tony raced home weekly to see it.

But Tony was, first and foremost, an athletics coach and mentor. He took that role seriously. He sacrificed hours and hours to help inspire and improve young athletes like me. Today, such mentoring isn't as visible, yet McKnight filled that gap for many young athletes over numerous years. Measuring his impact on my career, Annadale Striders, and

Northern Ireland athletics would be impossible. The fact is: Tony McKnight was in a league of his own and one of a kind. He remains a genuinely legendary character - someone who will never be forgotten.

Mary Peters.

Chapter Three - 'The Mary P'

1972, the year Mary Peters claimed gold in Munich, became the darkest year of The Troubles in Northern Ireland up to then. In what became known as Bloody Friday, the IRA detonated twenty-two bombs in 75 horror-filled minutes. The British Government had sent troops to the province to try and keep order. Peace lines and walls were erected to separate Catholic and Protestant communities in interface areas, but the violence continued and impacted every aspect of life, including sports.

No wonder that, following her exploits in Munich and her off-track life at work and home, despite the mayhem, having helped build a brand-new athletics stadium, Mary Peters eventually became Lady Mary Peters, a symbol of hope and unity. At that time, she had ignored the palpable danger on the streets of Belfast to help fundraise on the Protestant Shankill Road and the Catholic Falls Road for her new track.

It was situated at Malone on the southern outskirts of Belfast. It officially opened on April 19 (Easter Monday), 1976, fulfilling her dreams of seeing a tartan track built in Belfast after that gold medal success in the Pentathlon at the 1972 Munich Olympics. This track, which bears her name, is surrounded by 30 acres of beautiful woodland, and it made for an idyllic and unique athletics venue that still retains its showpiece setting today. Even though our training runs along the nearby River Lagan towpath were magnificent, they couldn't compare to the training sessions and races we experienced on the brand-new state-of-the-art facility.

RUNNING AWAY

People were ecstatic that such a marvellous resource was now on our doorstep. We constantly had to pinch ourselves!

Born in Liverpool, Mary Peters came to Northern Ireland as a child after her father had been relocated for work purposes. After her gold medal triumph in Munich, when she defeated the hot favourite for the Pentathlon, Germany's Heidi Rosendahl, not surprisingly, she quickly became a national treasure in Northern Ireland and Britain. Towards the end of the Seventies, 'the great Mary Peters', as she became affectionately known, was, to my delight, a guest of honour at our school, Gransha High in Bangor, following sports day.

Like the new South Belfast track, our school was also a brand-new state-of-the-art construction where I was fortunate to meet another of my early mentors and encouragers – my English teacher, Mr. Mairs. He spotted potential in me long before I saw it in myself. Mairs was tall, slim, and a little chaotic despite always wearing a clean shirt and tie, yet I remember feeling safe, welcome, and valued in his classroom. He regularly praised my essays and written work, even though he and I knew they could and should have been much better. Then, one day, out of the blue, he spoke what ultimately proved to be life-changing words to me.

'I believe you'll be a writer and author someday," he commented.
I was stunned and encouraged, and I didn't believe it.

The thought of becoming an author and writing books was so outlandish that I couldn't comprehend it. As I recall, "Mairsey", as he was known at our school, was one of the first people outside my family to take a personal and keen interest in me. If ever a man was chosen for the teaching profession, this gentle soul was. He refused to focus on my flaws or doubts, which were considerable; instead, he spoke powerful, positive words to help me achieve what might otherwise have proved impossible. He differed from some of the other teachers who considered our entire form a lost cause. Once, when we all arrived for a maths class, I recall how the teacher gasped, put his head in his hands and declared, "I forgot it was you lot!" I couldn't blame him. However, times have changed.

Despite Mair's keen interest in my schoolwork and constant encouragement, I was consumed with only one thing: my running goals. Flattered by his confidence in my writing ability, my yearning was still for athletics and sports. Helped initially by my sports teachers, David Bennett and Jim Barrett, I couldn't believe someone like Mary Peters had been chosen to hand out the prizes as our special guest at the time. I still remember the joy of receiving a winning medal from her in that packed assembly hall.

With her famous long, blonde hair, trademark smile, and softly spoken voice, she whispered, "Well done, John. Keep working hard at your event, and you can reach the stars." It is still one of my proudest moments and a day when life-changing words entered my ears. That warm summer day in a school assembly hall, packed with dreams of every kind, Mary Peters planted a seed that helped transform my life. She may not have realised it, but those early expressions of affirmation, when I was an impressionable youth lacking confidence and self-esteem, were not just what I needed to hear - they said, "I believe in you," and "You can succeed in life." Her words defied the province's agonies and ever-present dangers, pushing me to discover my true potential instead. She, more than most, recognised the importance of self-belief. In her 2023 autobiography, Mary Peters (My Story), she wrote, "It is trite to say that without believing in yourself, you can achieve nothing, but in my case, it took an agonisingly long time for that to sink in."

Of course, Lady Mary Peters led more than me in the right direction. She helped change the lives of numerous young athletes. Her enthusiasm and positivity massively impacted beleaguered and war-torn Northern Ireland. Since those early days, the Mary Peters Track has drawn more people with every passing year, and her Trust has supported over 4,000 athletes in search of their dreams. While on the international scene, Mary Peters, who has referred to herself as "an Ulster woman" even though she hailed from England, constantly acknowledged her people with positive words, notwithstanding the poor reputation Northern Ireland had in the Seventies due to the ongoing conflict. Even defying death threats, she courageously put her words into action by building a super stadium to unite people of all backgrounds, thus launching a significant turnaround in Northern Ireland's deteriorating political climate.

Subsequently, few would disagree that the Mary Peters Track became more than a mere athletics stadium; it became, in many ways, totemic, a beacon of light and a ray of hope from on high amidst the disorder. If ever a 'godsend' had arrived, it was the Mary Peters Track. She didn't only invite young people to her new facility; she urged them to stop throwing bricks and petrol bombs and start positively using their energy. They were encouraged to meet new friends from across the divide, bury the hatchet, and become a new generation's future leaders and legends through sport. It was subtle but brilliant. And, as we know today, such transformation would ultimately be experienced in Ulster. Yet, that hard-won peace and harmony began many years before at the beautiful, tranquil setting known as the Mary Peters Track in the late nineteen seventies and early nineteen eighties. Mary had become, in effect, her Track and her Trust.

Once the Track opened, Mary invited schoolchildren like me from all over the province to try out her new surface at Malone. What wasn't to like about that for children of 'The Troubles?' I will never forget my first few tentative steps around the new surface. I felt like I was New Zealand's John Walker in a top mile event or Sebastian Coe setting another world record. The soft tartan surface was incredible and much easier on my young, skinny, undeveloped legs. To understand the significance of this new state-of-the-art facility, before 'the Mary P' opened, I had been used to training on an old cinder one at Bangor's Ward Park that afterwards effectively left my legs feeling like they'd been run over by a bus. I loved

Ward Park, but was not too fond of that cinder track – those ashes! We could hardly see the white lines on the dark, grey gravel, which probably explained why there were often no disqualifications for running into another lane during events. And try running on it when it is wet? It was an era of trial and error when amateur athletics was precisely that – amateur! The coaches and officials were sincere and dedicated, but funding was scarce, and the facilities were far from ideal. So, imagine my relief when the opportunity arrived to glide over an impressive surface like the one eventually used for the 1976 Olympic Games in Montreal. We thought we'd died and gone to track heaven!

Meanwhile, despite the ongoing 'Troubles,' the Mary Peters Track still managed to draw many top athletes to the city and her new track and training ground. Brian Hooper pole-vaulted his way to a British record in Belfast, which set the scene for many incredible athletic events at the Belfast venue, thanks to the excellent work of the late Les Jones of the NIAAA. Those nights were vintage as thousands converged on Malone's enclosed circuit. Watching local 1500-metre expert Jim McGuinness break the 4-minute mile while taking on the world's best, like New Zealand's John Walker and Britain's Steve Ovett, gave hope to many younger athletes like me and was a thrilling experience.

Other top names like Ed Moses, Steve Cram, Zola Budd, Fatima Whitbread, Tessa Sanderson, and Northern Ireland legend Mike Bull graced the track over the next 20 years. 'Athletics Weekly' described Mike Bull in 2015 as 'Britain's greatest ever pole vaulter'. Capped no fewer than 69 times for GB and Northern Ireland, he won gold and two other silver medals at the Commonwealth Games, competed at two Olympics, and broke the British record 25 times before retirement.

Yet, like 'Mary P,' he remained a down-to-earth individual with a great passion for his sport and helping others, including me. When Mike opened a gym in my hometown of Bangor, it became a centre for aspiring young sportsmen and women, and anyone interested in health and fitness. Learning from and rubbing shoulders with such company was critical for my colleagues and me. The hardest part, however, wasn't lifting heavy weights but standing in shorts and a vest beside some of the top bodybuilders in Bangor – and Mike! Talk about humiliation! I was as thin as a rake and used to wait until they had gone home before daring to leave the changing rooms. Some days, I would sit in the sauna, get dressed again, and go home without completing a single bench press. That was a vintage period in Northern Ireland's sporting history and a welcome relief from the distress of our ongoing conflict at home, which, for many of our fellow citizens, had become an everyday anguish.

Mike's influence also helped propel me to another level. Quickly reaching junior international status and racing against the legendary Steve Cram in the World Junior Cross Country Championships and, on another memorable occasion, in the British Junior International, 1500 metres, was an unexpected privilege I experienced in those days. Of course, only years later did we discover how successful Steve Cram would become on the track. If I'd known I was racing against a future world mile record holder back then, I might have grabbed his autograph! After leaving runners his age and mine trailing in the 1500, it was apparent that the man nicknamed the 'Jarrow Arrow' was destined for greatness. He ran well under 3.50 that day while the rest of us fought it out around the 4-minute mark.

The only junior athlete who could get anywhere near Cram was a long-haired, ungainly Scottish sensation called Graham Williamson, who ran most of the race like a stray horse with his head bobbing up and down. Due to constant injury, people reckoned Williamson may not have reached his full potential. However, before he retired, he still recorded a respectable 3.50 for the mile, a Scottish record, and became a genuine thoroughbred in middle-distance running. Williamson's guts and determination were impressive, giving every race his all. Still, everyone knew 'Crammy' was a class apart and would one day likely break the world record for the mile, which he eventually did, recording a time of 3.46.32, a European record.

While my peers and I found it impossible to compete with a genuine athletics legend like Steve Cram or the equally impressive Williamson, I slowly began to progress. I finished well inside the top fifty in the World Junior Cross Country Championships, held at the Hippodrome de Longchamp on March 9, 1980. But that first international excursion to Paris became memorable for more than my performance. The sight of my shabby white suitcase with a massive handle was more akin to a cheap sewing machine rather than the property of a seasoned international sports competitor and traveller.

"Hurry up, McCreedy; you're late. Get that ugly contraption up here on the check-in," bantered one of the Northern Ireland coaches at Belfast International Airport.

The entire party was in hysterics. My fellow athletes skedaddled' due to the embarrassment as I entered the airport, holding the white eyesore with marked silver locks, but it didn't bother me. I had hardly slept a wink the night before. I was grateful for a free trip to Paris – suitcase spectacle or no! Arriving in Paris was equally amusing when we were met by a French security guard who assumed we spoke French. "What's wrong with you? Do you not speak the Queen's own English?" commented one of the Northern Ireland officials. The none-the-wiser security man hadn't a clue what he was saying.

When the race began, the runners had to steeplechase extremely high barriers, which unnerved many competitors and hindered me considerably in the early part. All these years later, I'm still incensed that no one told us about the barriers before the race began. I was so small I could hardly get over them. I wasn't a steeplechaser, just a runner. I didn't see this coming. I'm convinced I would have been placed even higher in the field without those barriers. I hadn't expected to compete in The Grand National, but that's how it felt. One of the fences was bigger than Becher's Brook! It wasn't fair!

Still, despite a slow and hesitant start, I came racing through the field to grab some notable scalps that day. I finished ahead of some exciting names, including the legendary Marcus O'Sullivan from Ireland, who would eventually break the four-minute mile over 100 times. I never finished in front of him again, though, and he almost lapped me in a 5000-metre race later that summer at Belfield, Dublin, bringing me back to earth with a bump. Back in Paris, I celebrated later that evening by downing more than a few bottles of Budweiser, which I don't think impressed the watching athletics officialdom.
But c'est la vie!

I was eighteen, and this was my first ever trip abroad. The world was my oyster at that stage – even Gay Paree, a city famous for its eternal fascination and celebrated mystique as the land of love and lovers. Lucky for some! My teammates and I failed to experience any of it. All I saw was bumper-to-bumper traffic as we travelled to and from the racetrack and got a distant view of the Eiffel Tower before beating it back to Bangor by sea, dragging that white, cringe-worthy sewing machine with us. I didn't disappoint on the world stage that day, but the airport was another matter due to that humble travel case.

Ultimately, the Mary Peters Track prepared me for big meets like the World Juniors and became a second home to me and many young athletes. It was a home from home and a place of relative safety during a distinctly unsafe period. I adored going there to train, even though it was a camel ride from our Bangor home. Thankfully, Coach McKnight arranged for me to be picked up and taken to 'the Mary P' three nights a week by Davy Smith – another of those early secret Samaritans and characters I probably took for granted during my youth.

"Smickers", as he was known to all of us, was a nightmare as a training partner because he could run the legs off you, but he was never as impressive on race day. I seem to recall how his car was not too reliable. He drove an ancient-looking Morris Minor on its last wheels, sounding like a tractor or low-flying helicopter. After collecting me, "wee Davy" would screech up to the lights in my hometown, and I would slide down below the car window just in case my friends spotted me at the top of our road. Sometimes, we pushed the car so much before training that we had no energy left. We used to pick up Brian 'Barney' Rowan in Holywood, who was carving up the track long before he became one of Northern Ireland's best-known political journalists. Back then, Barney was a talented 1500-metre runner, winning frequently, but you couldn't tell if he was pleased because his hair was so long no one could see his face.

Meanwhile, "Smickers" regularly drove Barney, me, and scores of other young athletes to training and races all over Ireland in that beat-up Beetle lookalike, sometimes not getting home until all hours of the morning. I recall one night how Davy could hardly drive back from Dublin for laughing after Mentor McKnight had asked me to pull up a chair and join the table at McDonald's on the famous O'Connell Street. The seat was one of those fixed chairs, and I kept yanking at it, almost breaking it. With the sweat dripping off me, my arms were in sheer agony! It took ages for the penny to drop. The rest of the Striders guys were in stitches. Talk about feeling stupid! McKnight was a master mischief-maker who loved playing tricks like that on his young prodigies, and I had fallen hook, line, and sinker for this one. Davy found it hilarious, too and reminded me about it for years afterwards. Once fed, we would stop at a little watering hole near Swords for a late-night tipple, and the craic, as they say, was mighty.

Sometimes, we only left for Belfast at around midnight. A local builder by trade, Smith was fearless on and off the track and possessed a heart like a lion. Despite all the driving and training, he would have to be up by 6 a.m. the following day to start a manual job. At the time, I think he lived in Dundonald, Co Down. He would bounce out of the front door to training, sporting the enthusiasm of a 5-year-old heading to the playground. Displaying such energy, I was convinced he was on something!

Despite the distance to the track from my home, however, and up to several visits per week, I don't recall him ever asking for petrol money. He loved his sport and helping others. He was one in a million! A genuine hidden helper if ever there was one. Come to think of it, neither did another of those early mentors and crucial helpers, Mike Roberts – a handy local sprinter at various distances, especially over 200 meters - ask my parents or me for anything. He, too, collected me on multiple occasions, and being considerably older and more communicative, I recall how he regularly challenged me not to forget my studies.

"What do you want to do with your life, John?'" he frequently asked me.
"Win an Olympic gold medal," was my response.
And if that isn't possible, what will you do?'" he would insist.

My blank stare told Mike everything he needed to know. I hadn't contemplated another life. I was super focused and could only think of sport, running, and those Olympics; the future seemed unimportant. My rose-coloured glasses couldn't envisage anything else.

Chapter Four - A Dance with Bridget

Growing up in Troubles-torn Ireland, opportunities were rare. Like any teenager in the thrills of youth, I was naïve, carefree, and often a little reckless. Yes, I was focused and dedicated to my chosen sport, but I was still a happy-go-lucky youngster who wanted to fly his kite. I would have believed and tried anything. In those days, I was constantly prone to rash and controversial decisions, a case in point being Bridget – my earliest memory of making a provocative choice that would not only rock the boat but almost sink it. During The Troubles, I'd had a few Catholic girlfriends, but none like Bridget. Mum frequently chased what she called 'The other sort' from our front door. She was convinced that I was bringing them home deliberately, which I wasn't. Unlike the other Catholic girls I dated, Mum had much more difficulty getting rid of Bridget. I became besotted with her.

Because of the polarisation in our communities, one day, my parents horrified me, demanding I finish with my beloved Bridget, a girl I had spotted at an Irish Dancing school. Even though she 'kicked with the other foot', as people used to say about someone from the opposite religion in Northern Ireland, it didn't bother me, but it gave my mum and dad nightmares. According to my anxious parents, we were from different sides of the tracks, I a Protestant and she a Catholic - and it wouldn't have worked out. They maintained I shouldn't have been anywhere near Irish Dancing anyway! It was the height of 'The Troubles.' Community tensions were at an all-time high and had affected the previous generation even more than mine. How on earth could I run for 'Ulster' and dance for Ireland?

My mother was a tap and ballet teacher, so what on earth was I doing at Irish dancing classes? She saw me as Fred Astaire, not Michael Flatley! In addition to her 'School of Ballet,' Mum had a boy's tap-dancing class, but I would never join. Attracting me were the female Irish dancers. These days, of course, Irish Dancing is known worldwide; it's an essential part of the heritage and culture of Ireland, just like the Irish Language, native sports like Gaelic Football, Hurling, Handball and Camogie, and traditional Irish music. Irish Dancing was around long before the legendary Michael Flatley and his spectacular revolutionary stage production 'Riverdance'. It features prominently at Irish-themed events like St Patrick's Day, Fleadhs, and All-Ireland and World Championships. And has spawned many 'variations on a theme' over the years.

Nevertheless, my community largely frowned upon the thought of a Protestant boy from a traditional unionist background skipping one, two, three, four, five, six, seven, and back in a pair of pumps, but I enjoyed it. I was even told I was good at it! Like the smooth clergyman Mr. Collins in 'Pride and Prejudice', I considered myself 'quite light of foot' in those days. Regarding Catholic girls like Bridget, my mother was convinced I was just too 'light of foot.'

In fairness, I don't think Mum's objections to Catholic girls like Bridget were solely political or religious. Other mixed marriages and relationships between Protestants and Catholics were felt not to have ended well, and she probably feared for my future as any good mother would.

Forbidden fruit or not, Bridget was the rosiest apple in the garden and, to me, the best-looking girl in Bangor. Irish Dancing was a small price to get close to her. By hook or by crook, I had to make it to those classes! My heart fluttering, I would cut through Bingham Street and High Street after school and skip down to the side door of the Royal Hotel on Bangor's seafront to get a glimpse of her. After pursuing her for some time, Bridget and I started seeing each other. Soon, my mother noticed small mysterious parcels landing in our hallway, but not from Royal Mail. Instead, after Bridget had visited the local shop, she would drop me in a range of sweets like '10p Mixes' and 'Lovehearts' through our letter box, accompanied by teen love notes, which infuriated my mother.

"Tell that wee dancer to stop littering our hall with those sweets", Mum would say. I stalked the letterbox obsessively, not for the sweets, but in case Mum beat me to it and read any of the notes. Some of them were borderline from Bridget. The sweets were unique. I loved the coconut-flavoured 'Jap Desserts,' especially the wee brown one. They don't make them like that anymore.

Meanwhile, Bridget's dad appeared to have many intolerances. "If you're heading out to see King Billy again, don't come back here tonight," Bridget's dad would threaten her. I never remotely saw myself as 'King Billy', but how others viewed you in those days was instructive, to say the least. He had alcoholism, while her mother seemed to me, at least, to spend more time at the chapel than at home. It was probably the only retreat open to her. She used to tell Bridget she had to repent twice – once for herself and then repeat the process on behalf of what she described as her "lost husband." Catholics, then, seemed to be constantly consumed with confession, which affected me. I imagined Bridget sitting and telling her priest all about us. God help him!

Bridget's mother was a lot softer at heart and good-looking like her daughter. When Bridget danced, she was a picture of her mum. I remember her fair hair, short green dress, black tights, and matching dancing pumps. She was a delightful girl who knew how to move, so I followed her around the Royal Hotel venue like a puppy dog, much to the annoyance of Maureen McCann, for many years a legendary Irish Dancing teacher in Bangor.

Maureen had discerned early on that my motives for being in her class had nothing to do with dancing. As if to confirm this, one night, I arrived home determined to announce my affection for my new Catholic girlfriend, leaving my parents horrified. Of course, when revealing their fondness for someone today, young people post on social media sites like Facebook or Instagram, saying, "I'm in a relationship with such and such." Back in the day, we just blurted it out to our friends and family like this: "I'm going out with a Catholic girl I met at Irish Dancing called Bridget. She's gorgeous."

Talk about a conversation-stopper!

My father, an Orangeman, almost choked on his tea that evening. Taking a long, drawn-out drag from his cigarette, he inquired: "What lodge does she walk with?" – a reference to which Orange Lodge she belonged.

RUNNING AWAY

"She walks alone," came Mum's sarcastic response.

Northern Ireland was incredibly divided in those days, and dark humour like my parents displayed was not unremarkable. Living close together since The Plantation or, as the saying has it in Northern Ireland, 'cheek by jowl', many people in Northern Ireland believed they could tell what background you came from just by knowing your name or, in some extreme cases, how you looked or how people acted or behaved. Catholics were called 'Fenians' and Protestants' Prods'. There was distrust on both sides. Even schools were easily identified by uniforms that screamed 'Green' or 'Orange.' There weren't many Catholic schools in Bangor then, so Catholics stood out like a sore thumb. Many Catholic children often received open abuse, which I felt was wrong and unfair. These poor souls were innocent of any wrongdoing, yet became scapegoats for the actions of republican paramilitaries. Maybe that's why I kept bringing home a stream of Catholic girls. They needed love and acceptance, and I was just the man to supply both! It's as good an excuse as I could then muster.

While my dad was a member of 'The Orange', he wasn't, to be fair, a 'staunch walker' or a 'true bigot' – to use Ulster expressions. He was much more tolerant. Like many Orangemen, for him, the Twelfth meant no more than a day at The Field, a traditional fish supper, and a few drinks. 'The Orange' was like a social club to him, somewhere to gather and relax and unwind from his work. My dad had more committee meetings than anyone I know, and they went on late! On reflection, he was the personification of balance, a man born to make a perfect First Minister of Northern Ireland. He could parade on the Twelfth with his bowler hat, collarette, shirt, and tie, sing 'The Sash', and then spend the rest of the night listening to Irish Folk music into the wee small hours in the front living room, surrounded by similarly progressive companions. I'm convinced he and his mates were visionaries for a New Ireland long before Sinn Fein or the SDLP advanced the idea, or any peace process had arrived!

Humour was vital to get us through a frightening period in our history, but there was still deep mistrust, and the constant threat of violence was a clear and present danger for Catholics and Protestants. In those days, we would hear of bomb scares, and sometimes they would come to nothing. It made us complacent. Then, the IRA was at its height, and the organisation had unleashed a bombing campaign on many towns and villages in Northern Ireland. In Bangor, we always felt more secure, even believing we were immune, but not on the day the bombs came to Bangor. I remember Mum and I getting caught in the panic. Following a warning, we sprinted down Main Street, unaware if a bomb would blow out into our path. We avoided the main Post Office and safely made it around the back of Market Street and home to our house. Although no one was killed or injured, the bombs later exploded in our beautiful Bangor and shook the town to its core. For our neighbours in nearby Belfast, however, this was sadly almost a daily experience.

Significant damage had been caused to various buildings on Bangor's Main Street. To witness the pictures of our wee town blasted in the newspapers the next day was hard to stomach. It made us angry, and we despised those determined to cause mayhem and destroy the country, especially our beloved Bangor. Until that awful day, we had always felt somewhat untouchable in Bangor, but no longer. For the first time, we knew how people in Belfast and other places felt. There was only a short journey between our seaside town and Belfast, yet we had never experienced violence in our own backyard. The closest we came before that was watching the latest news bulletin on TV.

"I can't believe we made it home. We were fortunate today, John," commented my shaken mother that day, who hugged us all after returning home. One thing is for sure: we were all on our knees that evening!

Although relatively sheltered from the almost daily reports of shootings and murders in Belfast, that day wasn't my family's or my only close shave during The Troubles in Bangor. Market Street still brings back memories of another lucky escape for my twin James and me. One evening, we had entered the lane leading up to Market Square when we were stopped by a gang of men asking us about our religion.

Pinning us to the wall, they asked: "Are you Catholics or Protestants?"

When someone asked that question during The Troubles, the motive was often sinister, especially at night, so we both froze. James and I knew the wrong answer wouldn't just mean elimination from the quiz shows 'The Chase' or 'Who Wants to Be a Millionaire.' It could mean a severe beating or shooting, leading to the loss of our lives.

I can only put it down to Divine inspiration and protection when I immediately countered, "We are neither. We are Christians."

"What's a Christian?" snarled the ringleader of the gang.

I didn't have a clue. I had never thought much about that question. We were both sent to church as young boys, and the minister regularly spoke about salvation and Christianity. The problem was I wasn't listening most of the time. I was too busy thinking of my Sunday dinner at my grandparents' house in Cotton, near Groomsport, where the fresh vegetables and tasty gravy were off the chart. Or dreaming about watching 'The Big Match' on Sunday afternoon, presented by the legendary and much-loved football commentator Brian Moore. If we were to shun the peril before us, I would need to draw on all those sermons by our minister to provide the correct answer – and fast!

Then, in the nick of time, the meaning of a Christian hit me like a ton of bricks.

"A Christian is neither Catholic nor Protestant," I said, adding, "A Christian has put their trust in God, had their sins forgiven and believes in the death and resurrection of Jesus Christ."

Billy Graham couldn't have put it better!

The gang was shellshocked and stared like they were offended. Looking at each other, they were uncertain what to do next until the ringleader snapped and pointed in the direction we had come—"Away you go," he said.

And go we did ... as fast as we could! Probably quicker than either of us had ever run. Our pulses were racing as we returned to the house and thanked our lucky stars that we hadn't ended up in Clandeboye Cemetery. To this day, it is a secret we didn't share with anyone, even our parents, as they would have been worried sick about us.

During the Sixties and Seventies, incidents like this were common and didn't always end so well. Stories abounded of people being victims of punishment beatings by one side or the other. "He or she just happened to be in the wrong place at the wrong time" was a well-known and tragic response. Peace walls kept many people apart and probably saved the lives of hundreds of others. Still, those walls hadn't been strong enough to separate Bridget and me – at least until someone finally squealed on us – a 'so-called' friend from around the corner, bringing our brief but beautiful relationship to an abrupt halt. I had ignored the advice and request from my parents to end things with my beloved Bridget from 'the other side of the track' until, one day, this friend of Mum's caught us courting in Ward Park. Spotting us from her bedroom window, she phoned my mother with the news. The lady lived close to the park and regularly kept an eye on us for Mum, which considerably restricted my teenage years.

What a tout!

"Did you say John and that wee Catholic girl had broken up, Winnie?"
"'Yes, they're well finished," replied Mum.

"Do you think so? I'm watching them smouching under the trees at The Park Bank, and they look very close to me. If you're not careful, Winnie, you'll have a Catholic baby on your hands," the lady responded.
A Catholic baby?

Babies are babies, but this was a C.A.T.H.O.L.I.C. baby!! Inconceivable! Incensed, Mum dropped the phone, grabbed a brush, sprinted down the lane into the park and up the bank and chased poor Bridget and me beyond the putting green to the park pond. I could run, but Mum could shift, too! She would have thrown us into that pond if she'd caught us. As Bridget escaped via the bridge towards the tennis courts, I screamed, "Run, Bridget, run,'" showing my loyalty to another female other than my mother for the first time, and to a Catholic girl, no less, which enraged Mum even more.

Even the tennis players put down their rackets to observe those afternoon shenanigans! My tennis days were over, at least at Ward Park. I could never go back there. I was mortified and disgusted, but not as much as when I arrived home that evening. Mum had produced that "sewing machine" –the horror case I had taken to Paris –packed it full of my belongings and dumped it onto the street. Cars were swerving to avoid it. Returning to the house, imagine my shock at finding it not on the doorstep but almost on the road.

It was lying 'half-open' as though it had been hurled in a fit of temper.

'True Love' had been replaced by what Mum saw as 'tough love.' My heart immediately sank. That big white case with all my stuff was all I had in the world, and the sight of it languishing there on the street would have been a wake-up call for any dependent and desperate teenager. It was a sobering experience; that moment, you realise you're still not ready for the big league even though you thought you were!

As it was, I was still utterly dependent on my parents for everything. I had nowhere to sleep, nowhere to go, and no choice but to part company with my childhood sweetheart and end my Irish Dancing days. I would never dance again the way I danced with Bridget. It became a case of what might have been partly because religion was and, sadly, still is, no laughing matter in Northern Ireland. People did what they felt they had to do to discourage mixed marriages, which today are much more common and accepted. Back then, however, such relationships were virtually no-go areas. So deep down, I knew I was beaten; my beautiful Bridget had to go. I had to cut ties. Running, not dancing, or dating would, of necessity, become my priority.

Chapter Five –

"Hello, John, it's America calling!"

By the Summer of 1980, the Olympic Games in Moscow had begun. Amid the Cold War tensions, those games became a political issue as much as a sporting event, with eighty nations present, including the United States of America, representing the smallest number since 1956. Sixty-six countries had boycotted the games entirely due to the Soviet-Afghan War. However, sport has frequently triumphed over politics, and this was no exception. Despite the odds, those controversial summer games still produced an epic and unforgettable battle between Britain's Steve Ovett and Sebastian Coe – two of the finest middle-distance athletes the world has ever seen.

RUNNING AWAY

The expectation surrounding the clash of these two athletic titans as to who would emerge the greatest was global. They broke world and national records for weeks before the event, but hadn't faced each other. Ovett was expected to win the 1500 metres, but he was victorious in the 800 metres. Then, in a remarkable turnaround of fortunes, Coe, who finished second in the 800, kept his nerve and produced a fantastic show of character and class to claw back and clinch gold in the 1500. The 800 was an epic encounter, remembered not only for the quality and unpredictability of the race but equally for the iconic sports commentary from the legendary David Coleman and that unforgettable line, "Steve Ovett, those blue eyes, like chips of ice." It made those Moscow games exceptional, but that's what great sports broadcasting does.

Growing up, I could never understand why my Nanda watched sports with the sound turned down. It used to drive me mad. When I asked him why one day, he replied, "I can see what's happening; I don't need someone to tell me." I couldn't have disagreed more. 'Atmosphere' makes watching sports exciting, but so does excellent commentary. Information is essential, and sports broadcasters who can produce spur-of-the-moment' one-liners ' are worth their weight in gold. Illustrious lines like "They think it's all over….it is now", said by Kenneth Wolstenholme when England won the World Cup in 1966, and "The Crazy Gang has beaten the Culture Club", said by John Motson after Wimbledon had shocked Liverpool in the FA Cup Final, spring to mind. I can still remember watching the World Snooker championships on TV during the 1980's. The legendary Steve Davis was at the table.

After he broke off and potted the first ball, everything went silent. As he made his way around the table, playing shot after shot, I hadn't heard a word from the commentator or the watching spectators, leaving me convinced there was a problem with the sound from my television. Maybe Nanda had crept into the room and turned it down! However, about 10 minutes into the frame, I remember finally hearing the voice of the great Ted Lowe say in his legendary soft tone: "The Master at Work." Lowe spoke in a whisper, which became his trademark. He didn't need to talk much again in that frame as Davis cleared the table. Four words only were required to put the icing on the cake on another exemplary performance from the king of snooker, Steve Davis. It was one of those classic moments in sports broadcasting. In Moscow, Coleman was also at his peak, but so were Coe and Ovett, who had done Britain proud, and their extraordinary exploits had helped put the sport of athletics firmly on the map.

From then on, only one thing dominated my thinking: I wanted to emulate them and become an Olympian. Winning a World or Commonwealth title is some achievement, but ask anyone in athletics: the pinnacle remains an Olympic gold medal. Every young athlete dreams of this. That summer, I would slip out of our modest home in Bangor and, overlooking the bay at Ballyholme, imagined winning gold like Ovett and Coe at the Olympics. I sat on a bench above the coastal path, dreaming of being aboard one of the boats heading up Belfast Lough or on one of the planes flying out of Aldergrove, our International Airport just North of Belfast.

Like all wannabe teenagers, the goal was to travel more, see the world, chase my dreams, and do something extraordinary with my life. I was born to run in more ways than one! I loved sitting on that bench, which is still there today. To the right is the picturesque harbour village of Groomsport. Over the water are Carrickfergus and Whitehead. Ballyholme is not for the fainthearted. No matter what time of the year, it can blow you away, but there's nowhere more beautiful in the world to walk, sit and wonder. The sight of Ballyholme Yacht Club, when the boats are in the water while the tide moves in or out, is breathtaking.

On that hill, looking out to sea, I always felt unbeatable. The sky was the limit. 'The Troubles' had offered no foreseeable hope to anyone. Many imagined escaping the nightmare in some form or another. It had provoked more than a feeling of failure and even embarrassment. What future would there be for young people like me in divided and war-torn Northern Ireland? Most of us wanted out of the place, and we wanted out fast. So, on top of that hill, I believed anything was possible. When Mum couldn't find me, she would send my brother or sister down to that bench, knowing I would be there daydreaming of a different life to the one I had been born into. Of course, this new and exciting life I desired would require passion, perseverance, and opportunity in spades, and I saw athletics as my passport. If you can dream it, you can achieve it, and like the strongest confirmation, that is what happened.

Out of the blue, that same summer, my ambition appeared to be realised when the chance of a lifetime suddenly landed following my return from Junior International duty.

Surprisingly, no fewer than nine airmails and offers from American universities came through our letterbox that summer, which astonished and delighted my family and me. "You've received another airmail, John", shouted Mum to my bedroom. The requests just kept coming, and I was speechless. I attracted attention from well-known colleges such as the Universities of Idaho, California, Texas, Oklahoma, South Carolina, Minnesota, Arkansas, Southern Illinois, and Rhode Island.

Of course, most young students would have taken time and space to decide which college best suited them. Their parents would have made suggestions, and meticulous preparation would have been the watchword.
Not me! I was fascinated by one of those letters, which had grabbed my attention from the get-go more than all the rest. When I opened that envelope, there was only ever going to be one result and one winner – my signature on the offer of a four-year athletic scholarship. So, before I had time to consider others, I made a choice that would soon come back to haunt me – a choice that would change the shape of my future - the decision to join the track team at West Texas State. I was so determined to go there, I couldn't wait to tell the other colleges I was sorted. Notwithstanding, I had unwittingly opened a Pandora's Box.

But why did I plump for West Texas?

And why so impatient?

Behind every decision, there's usually a dominant goal, and I had one.

That said, I didn't need to rush. I'd received much better offers than West Texas that summer. I had set my heart on becoming the next Coe, Ovett, Cram, and closer to home, Eamonn Coghlan, or John Treacy and would have been wise to take my time about where I should study and train for my ultimate dream – to run in the Olympics. Eamonn Coghlan and John Treacy were athletes who were elite middle and long-distance runners and genuine heroes of mine.

Like many aspiring Southern Irish athletes then, they were based in America. Lurgan-based Jim Haughey and I were among the privileged Northern Irish runners who had the opportunity to follow them. Having finished ahead of five Scottish athletes, five runners from the South of

Ireland, and the complete Welsh team at the World Juniors, Bob Amato, who coached John Treacy at Providence in Rhode Island, approached me to see if I would be interested in going to America.

Coghlan, from Dublin, was at Villanova University in Pennsylvania for four years. An outstanding exponent over a mile, indoors and outdoors, he won a World title at 5000 meters in 1983. Coghlan became legendary there, along with some of the best milers in NCAA history, such as Ronnie Delany, Marty Liquori, and Jumbo Elliot. Treacy from Waterford, at Providence, was a prolific road and cross-country performer, winning the World Senior Cross-country event held in Limerick, on the west coast of Ireland, in 1979, where I competed in the Junior race the same year. The course was a swamp, and only the fittest survived. The event was staged at the GreenPark Racecourse on 25th March 1979, and the sight of athletes rather than horses running around the white posts was striking.

Like me, Treacy was exceptionally lean in frame, and instead of sinking, he glided over the muddy ground as if it wasn't there. No one could touch him. He was impressive, rugged, and highly talented. On that memorable day, he flew to World Championship glory to the delight of the thousands of watching Irish fans, none more so than me. I was ecstatic as people clapped and threw their hats into the air. Imagine an Irishman had become the world cross-country champion in his home country, leaving hope for us all! I was from Northern Ireland, and Treacy was from The South.

I grew up being told I was British, not Irish, but that day in Limerick, there wasn't a prouder and more emotional Irishman than me. It was probably when I realised I am Irish and will always be. I love to see the Irish Rugby team win and the Ireland soccer team, except when they play Northern Ireland! I am Irish through and through. Abraham Lincoln once said, "I like to see a man proud of the place in which he lives. I like to see a man live so his place will be proud of him."

While I wanted achievements similar to John Treacy's and saw him as the perfect role model, I was equally conscious that athletics was about more than running. The opportunity to go to America would also allow me to succeed in life and achieve my childhood dreams, but again, why Texas, and why the sudden hurry? Was bettering myself the sole motive for going to America? Thanks to the local Press, interest in me from

RUNNING AWAY

America soon became public knowledge. So, sitting comfortably in our front living room one afternoon, my hysterical sister burst in with the breaking news that would change my young life. I had known about the scholarship interest but didn't think the Press would report much about it, so I wasn't expecting what Jillian had uncovered.

"Quick, John, Mr Rankin says your photograph is in the paper tonight."

"You're having me on; the paper comes out at the weekend," I answered. I had been referring to the weekly edition of 'The Co Down Spectator,' a newspaper that regularly reported on local news, sports, and my progress. But my sister was talking about the national evening paper, 'The Belfast Telegraph,' then Northern Ireland's leading newspaper and only evening one.

"You're kidding me, sis. Me, in 'The Tele?' 'The Belfast Telegraph?' It can't be true!"

"If Mr Rankin says it is true, it must be because when it comes to 'The Tele,' he misses nothing. Hurry up, John, get down to the shop and grab a copy."

I had made the national press, which was the first time I probably felt I must be making progress in my chosen sport. I had lots of press cuttings from my local paper stored in a scrapbook, with many trophies in our cabinet at home, but something about this moment made me feel that athletics wasn't just some hobby but a potentially full-time business. The little green V-neck sweater with a white shirt made me look more like an amateur golfer or tennis player, not an athlete. But fame was fame!

John Rankin was our legendary friendly neighbour, a regular reader of the evening paper and a font of knowledge. We all adored him. Every night in life, he would stand with his companions for what seemed like ages outside the local newsagents, 'The Pandora' on Hamilton Road, waiting for the arrival of the latest edition of 'The Telegraph'. The very name Pandora still brings back happy memories for me. I loved buying Toffee Crisps and pens there.

I have lost count of the Toffee Crisps I have eaten and the pens I've bought over the years. When I began to write, my fascination only increased. I borrowed them from countless people. Though not always consciously, I've also walked off unconsciously with numerous pens from people. I don't particularly like those thin little ballpoint pens, which break easily. I am more interested in a good, solid writing pen, but if I am desperate, I will use anything.

I love pens and need them for work, so when it comes to ink, I can't help myself. I have this overwhelming terror that I will be left with no pen, so I always keep them close. Once, when I had what looked like a forest of pens in my top jacket pocket, a colleague at work asked, "Is that really necessary?" It was a fair question. So, you've been warned; if you have a pen and are around me, guard it with your life!

Meanwhile, following a day's work and having purchased 'The Tele,' John Rankin would stroll back up the street, whistling and beating that same edition against his leg like someone with nothing better to do. It always seemed boring to me, but Rankin was among the most content and likeable men I can ever remember meeting. His daily 'Hello' made our childhood more bearable. He was also great fun.

It's America Calling.

"Is your name Sean?" he would ask me, provoking the response, "No, it is John."

"Is it Seamus they call you, boy? He would ask my twin, provoking another sharp response. "No, it is James."

In those days, calling two Protestant youngsters in Northern Ireland,

'Sean' and 'Seamus,' was bold and sure to get a reaction, yet no matter how often he jested, we continued to fall for it. He had two sons, Billy and Norman. Billy was a gifted sportsman, especially at tennis, while Norman was a respected goalkeeper who, like me, didn't like losing.

Speaking of talented sports stars, our town of Bangor punched well above its weight when producing homegrown sports talent. Northern Ireland has an incredible sporting history, generating world-class performers in various sports. Many of the country's leading sports people have hailed from Bangor, and some lived around the corner from me. Our town knew how to churn them out.

Glenn Thompson, a close neighbour from Castle Street, was a talented tennis player and footballer who played in the Irish League with Linfield and Bangor. Chris Fleming and Peter Dixon joined English football clubs Wolves and Stoke City, respectively. Terry McMaster, Mark McCall and Don Whittle played rugby for Ulster and Ireland.

At the same time, I recall with some frustration how the late Sean Millar, a fellow Northern Ireland International athlete, taught me a lesson in the Bangor Road races one Saturday afternoon by leaving me trailing over 10,000 metres. He was on fire that day; no matter how well I ran, I couldn't close the gap. I could mention many more talented sports people from the town, like Formula One ace Eddie Irvine, cyclist Alistair Irvine, and golfer David Feherty. I would require two books to include all the different names. Many of our sports were played at Bangor's Ward Park. It was where we learned our trade. Yet, for reasons I know not, there was only one boy in our street who seemed to own a decent football; the problem was that when a penalty decision went against him, he would lift the ball and take it home with him.
Game over!

I still remember us begging him to bring the ball back out. We would flatter him about how he was the best goalkeeper in the world, even offering to award him the penalty he felt robbed of, a new pair of goalie gloves, potato crisps, and Coke, but to no avail. He was in for the night! Mind you, I'd probably have done the same if the penalty had gone against us and I had owned that ball.

Meanwhile, John Rankin may have been joking about our names but it soon became clear he wasn't kidding about my newfound prominence as an athlete. When I picked up the paper that night, there it was. In black and white – "Hello, John, it's America calling", read the headline. I had to look twice. There was also a photograph of me, which had been taken sometime earlier by 'The Belfast Telegraph', with the parted Eighty's hairstyle, holding the telephone in our home. Giving the impression I was speaking to a posse of top universities in the States, which, of course, I had. I was shocked, however, at the attention I was receiving. I suppose I never expected 'The Telegraph' to run the story. It was too good to be true! And so, unfortunately, it seemed, was America at that stage.

Chapter Six - JR, Southfork, and Choices

Overnight, the scholarship interest propelled me from an unknown athlete to a rising sports star, producing a natural feel-good factor for any eighteen-year-old. I didn't require top grades to enter exciting colleges – a welcome relief! The universities seemed more interested in my athletic ability. My obsession with sports, specifically athletics, had always hindered my studies. However, I still had to sit a test at Trinity College in Dublin. My mother had bravely driven me there - the first time she had ventured outside Bangor in a car. She was even more nervous than me. Mum had taken up driving later in life and knew nothing about operating outside a 5-mile radius. By the time we reached Dublin, we were screaming at each other. Mum was a bundle of nerves on the road, and I was a bundle of nerves about the test. It was a recipe for war, and war ensued! How we ever made it to Dublin and back remains a mystery.

In those days, there was no M50 North and Southbound. I remember how we couldn't make head or tail of the signs in the South. There was no toll road or easy route to Dublin from the North. At the Border, we had to pass the Bureau de Change, a petrol station, an army checkpoint, the Irish Customs, not to mention the endless queues of lorries and trailers. The main roads were dreadful. Huge craters greeted us, and I don't know how the car's tyres survived.

We had to drive through Dundalk, the dreaded Drogheda, and Balbriggan before hitting 'The Big Smoke' and Dublin City. Drogheda was the most challenging place for any motorist travelling from North to South. It was the 'Mother of all Bottlenecks' - always crammed with vehicles. Sometimes it took longer to get through the town centre than it did to make the journey from Co Down. But we made it... eventually. It was, in effect, a driver's nightmare.

Despite our frequent clashes, Mum was not just a star but another one of those early helpers who played such a valuable part in my story.

Without her, I would not have gained the opportunities I did. I recall how her eyesight wasn't the best, not improved by her refusal to wear glasses. No surprise then when she ran over a roundabout at Dundalk on the way home that night and continued as though nothing had happened! It was like something out of the TV Comedy, 'Only Fools and Horses.' I couldn't wait to get home, and when we finally arrived, the sight of Belfast Road in Bangor was some relief. Despite doing me a huge favour, something I would always be grateful for, I vowed never to travel long distances with her again, and I kept to that!

Nevertheless, Mum's love and support back then were not just crucial in helping me realise my sporting dreams; they became a sustaining influence for the rest of my life. Love must be expressed during the earliest and formative years for a child to thrive physically and emotionally in later life, and I was blessed with both.

Cheered on by the love of a mother, my progress on the track would soon present me with an impossible choice - one with even more significant concerns than finishing with Bridget. No one had reminded us more about the importance of our choices than Mum. She would repeat how decisions have consequences. "Life is all about choices, which determine much about our futures – they are never straightforward," she insisted. "Never underestimate the importance of your decisions," she had drummed into her children. "Your choices will either make or break you," Mum claimed. She insisted her own life had taught her this, and I was just about to find out how accurate she was.

Before marrying my father, Mum had lived in Canada, in Toronto, and although only a teenager, she had found love with a boy called Tom. He was Canadian, and she adored him as much as he idolised her. They eventually became engaged, much to the horror of my grandmother or 'Nanny' as we affectionately called her. Nanny was something else! She used to bring us Milky Way chocolate bars from the Bangor market every Wednesday and made the best custard ever! However, while Mum was still a teenager, Nanny and our Nanda had returned to Northern Ireland from Canada to begin a new life.

When my mother refused to join them, Nanny became awkward and distant from her for almost a year. According to Mum, Nanny cried tears, stamped her feet, and used various forms of manipulation to try and end Mum's relationship with Tom, but her efforts failed. After arriving home, she even wrote emotional, weekly begging letters to my mother, pleading with her to return to Ireland. "There's a job waiting here for you, Winnie," she would pen: "I've spoken to several people willing to get you fixed up. You'll love it here." Nanny had also gone so far as to have someone who would eventually become my dad waiting in the wings for Mum at a British Legion dance hall.

The control was off the chart, but Mum held firm and said she couldn't return.

Then 'Nanny' ramped things up a gear, suggesting she couldn't continue without her daughter. "My life isn't worth living if you're not around," she would write, adding: "I've become very unwell and don't know how long I have left." She was still a relatively young woman, but Mum was concerned. Naturally, under this tirade of torment, she soon began to wilt. The writing was on the wall for poor Tom. He begged her not to go home. "You'll never come back here", he pleaded.

"Of course, I will, " Mum insisted, but in her heart of hearts, she knew it wasn't true. Confronted by a terrible dilemma, Mum suddenly faced a devastating choice between family duty and true love.

Consequently, Mum agreed to come home for what was supposed to be a 'short holiday' but predictably never returned to Canada. In many ways, Mum's story wasn't unlike that of Eilis Lacey, played by Saoirse Ronan in the fantastic 2015 movie 'Brooklyn'. The only difference was that Mum would have no fairytale ending. Ellis Lacey returned to her true love in America, but Mum never set foot in Canada again. Nanny had worn her down and got her way. That would probably not happen today. Young people are much stronger and more independent. It was a different story then. Young people were possibly more conscious of their parents' wishes, much more cooperative and, perhaps, at times, afraid. So, Mum's Canadian romance inevitably ceased from there on. She said she never regretted having her children in Ireland, but she found it hard to excuse her mother for interfering at such a crucial stage in her life. Mum was forced to make a meaningful life choice against her heart, which is always a recipe for regret. Ultimately, the decision broke Tom's Canadian heart and left Mum wondering what might have been for the rest of her life.

Ah, yes, choices!

In the summer of 1980, after accepting a brief and regrettable phone call from America, I made a similar life choice regarding my sport – one that I would regret, at least initially. That call I'd received from America continued to trouble me for some time afterwards. If only I had been out at the time.

If only I had been a little older and wiser.

If only I had let the phone ring.

If .....only.

Hindsight is a wonderful thing! But this call caught me off guard because it appealed to other desires within me outside of athletics.

"Hey, I'm the head coach at West Texas State. May I speak with a young athlete called John McCreedy, please?"

My heart stopped. Did he mention Texas?

"Speaking," I said. "Did you say you were from Texas?"

This man didn't realise he was about to strike oil easier than a Dallas-style Barnes/Ewing hit. There would be no need to impress his student target with chatter about excellent facilities or other amenities in the way many US coaches go to extraordinary lengths to land athletes or football stars in the making. However, he still poured on the charm like all good recruiting American coaches, and before long, I was eating out of his hand.
"'Yes, I'm from Texas. I'm just calling to see if you received our track scholarship offer, John. Have you heard much about Texas?" the coach continued.

"Heard of it? I've thought of nothing else since JR and 'Dallas' appeared on our TV screens. I'm glued to it each week," came my excitable response.

Quickly realising my fascination with all things Ewing, the coach must have thought it was his birthday, and from then on, it was.
I was "toast."

Of course, West Texas State is a long way from Dallas, where my TV heroes were stationed – a difference of around 400 miles, as it happens - but I didn't know that, then. Once I heard the word Texas, it was game over! I assumed I would be joining the Buffaloes – the nickname for West Texas Sports - and heading off to some part of that great state, which was good enough for me. I required no further persuasion from the coach, even though he was dying to offer it.

'The Blind Side' is a film about a rising football star named Big Mike who is courted by countless universities in America and gets offered all sorts of incentives to join their football team, including nights out and being treated to the best American chicken. Even his adopted kid brother, SJ, is presented with the chance to lead out the team Mike signs for, flip the coin, and play a sideline pass. That's standard protocol when trying to bait a talented athlete in America. But in my case, no such inducement was needed, just some light encouragement and small incentives. It was the easiest sell in town for the coach, but not for reasons you might assume. My motives for choosing Texas had little to do with athletics or study.

"What do you like about the soap 'Dallas,' John?" added the coach.

"I sit all week waiting for it. I've never seen such a wonderful place. You can be in the city for one minute and on a horse with the cattle in the countryside next. It looks like a fantastic place to live. Besides, that guy JR is something else, isn't he? What a man!"

"He sure is all of that, " replied the coach.

J R was hardly a good role model for any young person, but, as we say back home, I lapped him up - and Dallas too. For Larry Hagman's legend of JR soon became TV gold with his "up to no good" tricks. Inevitably, the smash-hit TV series 'Dallas' proved incredibly popular with all age groups during the late Seventies and early Eighties, delivering a welcome escape from the dark, cold, wet, and miserable winter days in Ireland and Britain while providing no shortage of drama thrown in. Ireland, after all, is an island in the North Atlantic!

What impressionable teenager wouldn't have been swayed by the allure of such a place? Okay, I would never get to swim in the Ewing pool or ride in Bobby's Mercedes, but training in Texas every day? Come on! How good could it get? I was more accustomed to blustery winds and bitterly cold mornings at Ballyholme than to those tempting tropical temperatures in Texas. When it came to the show, I loved the theme music, which ended in a pitched tone and dramatic fashion, just like each episode. It left me on the edge of my seat, and I couldn't wait until the following week to watch the next episode.

The American prime-time TV soap aired on CBS from April 2, 1978, to May 3, 1991. The affluence and constant feuding in the Texas family, known as the Ewings, caught the eye, but it was JR, played by Larry Hagman, who stole the show with his legendary scheming and dirty business deals. JR was the only character to have appeared in every episode, and who will ever forget the cliffhanger event in 1980, known as "Who Done It" or "Who Shot JR" – the second highest-rated prime-time telecast ever. With its 357 episodes, Dallas remains one of American history's longest-lasting, full-hour prime-time TV dramas. Is it any wonder I couldn't believe I was about to be offered the opportunity to set foot in Texas? More than anything, that influenced my decision to reject every other offer and plump solely for West Texas. My decision wasn't from my head but from my heart, which can often prove catastrophic, and this was no exception.
"Okay, listen up, John. We'll fit you out on arrival with a big old cowboy hat like JR. You can also ride a few horses in Texas and sample some great American burgers. How does that sound, young man? " countered the head coach.

"Oh, really, that would be a dream and so neat", I replied, sounding more American than him even though I had never set foot on American soil.

"Can I go to the Oil Barons Ball, too?" I asked, unable to separate fiction from reality. Do you think I'm joking? The coach quickly sensed this Dallas obsession with his potential signing. A seasoned operator, he was well-schooled in flattery and knew when to go for the kill.

"John, your life will be a ball from here on. We appreciate quality here at West Texas, and for you, the sky is the limit; you can go to those Olympics, young man, if you want to. We want you, we believe in you, and we will make you a star."
Before the head coach could finish, I remember yelling the words he had probably longed to hear – "I have already signed the contract, coach." Ecstatic at the prospect of being in Ewing territory, sun worshipping at Southfork, and watching Lucy, Sue Ellen, and Pammy enter the pool, Texas had no rivals regarding my signature. In my imagination, I was already on my way to the Lone Star State. I was as good as gone. From having lunch with Jock and Miss Ellie to sharing a drink with good old Cliff Barnes in one of those fancy downtown restaurants, it was a case of Dallas; here I come!

My only question was, "How soon?"

"Are you kidding, John? If you return the forms, we'll have you here before you know it. We will sort out all your travel details and be in touch," I was assured.

I fell to the floor, yelled a huge thank you, and screamed - "Yes!!!"

On hearing the news, James and Jillian were elated, but to my shock and horror, Mum didn't buy it; neither was she happy, and I could sense it. She'd been listening in and thought it was all too smooth. Nothing beats experience, and Mum had plenty of it. I was no match for the wily coach. I was a naive and impressionable youngster with no worldly experience. I was out of my league, and she knew it.

"I'm not convinced, son. You know nothing about this place, and that man sounds far too nice to be true. I'm not comfortable with this," maintained Mum.

"Don't be so negative, Mum. I'm heading straight to Southfork. Have you seen the girls over there? It's a done deal; I'm away to America."

"Grow up," she snapped. "There are pretty girls in Ireland, too.

RUNNING AWAY

Don't be fooled by a TV soap, big houses, and fancy cars. Your motives are wrong, John. You wanted to run and train for the Olympics, not chase after girls, and become JR Ewing. Did the coach offer you a full scholarship?
It was a fair point!

Mum reminded me that we couldn't afford a full scholarship. Anyway, regarding my impetuousness, she was right. Perhaps I had dived in too quickly? I had sold the ranch for a song, and what if it all went pear-shaped? I was so excited about getting to Texas, I hadn't even been listening or concentrating. Just what was being offered to me? I had a verbal promise, but nothing else. I had a gentleman's word but no contract. I had lots of overtures but no guarantee. Yet, impulsively, for reasons I cannot explain, I informed other interested colleges, including many better ones than West Texas, that I would not, regrettably and respectfully, be able to accept their kind offers. I remember painstakingly writing those letters one after another and posting them myself. Even the uneasy feeling in my stomach failed to dissuade me from this course of action. "Listen to your gut" is an old expression, but I refused to take note on this occasion. I was completely deluded by the thought of training in Texas and seeing in the flesh the cast of my favourite TV show. Oh, the naivety of youth!

I kept imagining myself being driven through the large gates of Southfork and arriving at the front door of that extraordinary American estate. I wouldn't know where to start, the pool, the house, or even the fields full of cattle.

Declining those other impressive and exciting invitations was risky, but Texas had no rivals in my world. It wouldn't have made the slightest difference if its competitors had offered me the sun, moon, and stars. Even if Villanova had come calling, I had only one thing in mind - training in Texas, visiting JR and Bobby at Southfork, and maybe, just maybe, being lucky enough to check out cute little Lucy, Pam, and Sue Ellen in their bathing suits! I should be so fortunate! Following that single call to our modest home in Bangor, I had booked the trip of a lifetime - my ticket to a mansion and a life I had only ever dreamed of. My road to riches and renown was settled after one brief conversation, and my spikes were packed. I was swapping Baltic Bangor for sweltering Texas. And nothing, not even my pessimistic Mum, could stop me.

Chapter Seven - Silence Isn't Always Golden.

They say silence is golden, but not when waiting for the most important letter of your life. Days passed, followed by weeks, and I was beside myself with worry and no word from West Texas State. Nada. No phone call, fax, or posted letter. No interest. Period!

The summer had come and gone, and my dream move to Texas was hanging by a thread. Most of my friends had received their exam results and secured college and university places. Some had left weeks before. I remained in limbo. Waiting for the postman each day on that all-important delivery was agonising. Where would I be flying into? Who would be collecting me? What day would I be starting officially? Those questions remained unanswered. Standing at the top of our street, I would watch for anyone in a red Royal Mail uniform carrying a sack full of letters. It was the early 1980s, and we didn't have the luxury of social media or the advanced communication available today. People had to wait to receive a letter and, in some cases, a telegram.

A Royal Mail airmail then was today's email or WhatsApp message. One day, I spotted red advancing towards our house and became excited. Finally, I thought to myself, my red-letter day had arrived. The postman had made it to our home. My ship had come in. I could relax and celebrate at last. Until I noticed my neighbour George McCoubrey wearing a Liverpool shirt, which upset me more. George, who lived down the street from us, was a brilliant goalkeeper who once saved six penalties in one game but never made the football grade. I have never been able to understand that. George's dad was an ardent Liverpool fan and a great swimmer. He would swim in the sea at Bangor seafront even on Christmas Day. Cold water didn't bother him. I could never gasp why! But at least he seemed to have the good sense to avoid Pickie Pool.

I remember how 'George Senior' used to chase me through the supermarket in Bangor to tease me about how Liverpool had beaten Everton yet again. Once, when I spotted him and hid behind a counter, he waited for his moment, popped his head around the corner, and taunted me like a schoolboy, but it was great fun.

Meanwhile, like a lovestruck teenager longing for a long-lost message from some sweetheart who'd long since disappeared, I was desperate to be handed my ticket to the USA, but, day after day, I was left disappointed. When I arrived home with another 'Sadsack' look, Mum consoled me, saying: "Don't worry, the letter will be here soon, son." The increasingly worried look on her face conveyed a different story. For I was very much down in the dumps. Compounding the issue was the fact that every time I ventured out the door, I would be stopped by friends and well-wishers and asked, "When are you leaving for the land of the free, John?" "We heard you're off to America; you must be super excited?" Unable to answer those questions, it became an immense embarrassment, yet the worst was still to come. Those earlier words from my mother echoed in agony through my head – "I'm not convinced, son." "That man sounds too nice to be true."

Why are mums always right?

Sensing my hurt and disappointment, my thoughtful sister Jillian consoled me: "Don't worry, John. You tried to do the decent thing by telling the other colleges you were sorted, which gave them time to find another athlete for their teams. That was, after all, the proper thing to do, wasn't it?" She was always such a sweetheart, but what she'd said wasn't entirely true.

Before I could answer, my twin interrupted.

"No," he replied. 'It was very naive to put all his eggs in one basket. Why couldn't he have waited a little longer? He didn't need to burn his bridges so quickly and absolutely!"

"Er, you can speak directly to me, James," I suggested.

But James was spot on. Why had I burned all my bridges? Why had I said no to all the other colleges, some much better known than West Texas? I hadn't decided with my head but with my heart. What a mess I'd created! It seemed like it was indeed all my fault. It was a worrying and awkward time for the family and me.

Stubbornly, however, I continued to make excuses for West Texas. "The coach and the college have more people to consider than me. I'm not the only athlete they've signed this year, " I countered.

Yeah, right! Who was I kidding?

One of my local rivals, Jim Haughey, an excellent distance runner from Lurgan, attended Clemson University in South Carolina, a college I might have accepted. Yet, I had turned down everything for West Texas. They owed me something. Notwithstanding, I still presumed, with patience, that the red-letter day would arrive, as Mum had assured me. Like a man who knows the game is up, I clung to the ridiculous notion that I was still on course for America and believed I was destined for the bright lights of Dallas. I lived on a fantasy island, afraid to face the music. And so, eventually, my mother insisted I call West Texas, expressing genuine concern about why I hadn't heard from the university.

Previously, I had stubbornly refused to call. Not because I wasn't keen to find out what was happening. My instinct told me there was a last-minute snag. That there was something up. And that I couldn't bear to face the truth. I would be horrified if America failed to happen. How would I tell my friends and colleagues? What would happen to my sporting career and reputation? I would become a laughingstock. Such thoughts tormented me. In my mind, the entire country knew I was leaving for America... everyone except me. At that time, one of my favourite songs was a late Seventies hit by American singer-songwriter Stephen Bishop. It was called 'On and On, On and On' – appropriate, given that my West Texas saga continued for months, not weeks.

RUNNING AWAY

To make matters worse, I had, at that time, completed a lengthy TV package with Leslie Dawes. He was a well-known sports reporter for Ulster Television, our local commercial TV station, filming me running at the Mary Peters Track for supposedly the final time before my athletic term in the States started. In his younger days, Dawes was a professional footballer in the Football League and played for his home-based club, Norwich City. He became interested in broadcasting, first on the radio, before joining UTV during the 1960's. Dawes was probably younger than he appeared, with thinning hair and a practical dress sense. He was friendly and encouraging. I recall how fussy he was in getting things perfect and how he insisted on what I considered pointless retakes that afternoon. It seemed to waste half the day and left my frustrated mother and me wondering why it took so long. I wasn't a world-beating athlete. I was an eighteen-year-old aspiring runner. My mother had driven me to the track that day, and I remember her asking, "What on earth is that man doing?"

I wondered myself. Mum had a dinner to prepare for the rest of the family, and her patience was thin. However, he was diligently doing his job, and the final package proved this, as it turned out well. Soon, my friends and athletic companions saw the TV report and sent cards to our home, wishing me every success in the States. If only they'd known about my scholarship woes; I had kept the silence from West Texas a closely guarded secret and hadn't revealed the mess to anyone, neither to friends nor especially the press. The evening national news was reporting on a young athlete from Northern Ireland being given the scholarship of a lifetime to the United States.

In contrast, that same young athlete had no written confirmation of anything. Bottom line: unless a miracle occurred, I knew I wasn't going anywhere, let alone America, and that a 'good news' story about the fortune of a young man swapping the town of Bangor for the US of A would go down like a damp squib

It was quite a burden for a teenager, but I had no choice but to endure it. Sleep deprivation followed, and my legs felt like jelly as I went for a run. Even the regular spoonful of honey I consumed failed to ignite a spark in me. I was addicted to honey in those days. Taking it regularly made a massive difference in my energy levels, but not then. Perhaps my love for honey had something to do with McKnight referring to me as a bumblebee!

A problematic period: I knew time was up. Coach McKnight agreed with my mother and compelled me to make the dreaded phone call, no matter how hard it would be. He had repeatedly used illustrations and analogies, some of which were legendary to our group of athletes! And, on this occasion, he provided another: "When someone is waiting on results from the doctor about a suspected illness, he can either go and hear what they are or bury his head in the sand. It is not always bad news, so make the call, John. You never know what will happen. It is better to know the truth than stumble around in the dark. If they don't want you, tell them to...." There were no back doors to our Tony!

While delighted that I had received my American dream, deep down, Tony didn't want me to go to the States as my leaving meant he would be minus one of his home-grown prodigies. He wouldn't have stood in my way, of course, never in a million years, but I think he saw the prospect of keeping me on board in Ireland when the American trace went cold. The silence from America affected him and Annadale as much as my family, hence his eagerness to resolve the matter. He genuinely cared about my welfare, and he demanded clarity.

Then, the dreaded moment of truth. Knowing I had no alternative, one early August afternoon, I plucked up the courage and made that fearful phone call. With Mum at my side and the rest of my family gathered around me and praying for good news, the scene resembled a man being anointed with oil by a group of ministers at an evangelical rally rather than a student phoning to see if he had been accepted to college. I can still recall my little sister sitting on the stairs with her hands clasped and the warmth from my brother's hands on my shoulders. God bless them!

Years earlier, I had competed against one of Northern Ireland's top cross-country exponents from Downpatrick, Tom Breen. Eventually, we became great rivals and friends. An Irish School champion and top-class cross-country performer, I recall being shocked to see him surrounded by his team and a priest and receiving prayer before his races. At the time, I had laughed it off as slightly over the top. "Is he being prayed for? It's only a running race, for heaven's sake," I would mock under my breath, but secretly, I was impressed with the duty of care he received and even a touch envious. After all, I would have to face the elements alone, while Tom Breen appeared to be seeking divine assistance.

In my front hall, I wished, like Tom's priest, that my local minister had joined my family circle of prayer partners as I plucked up the courage, picked up the telephone, and dialled the number to America. Huddled together, it seemed to take forever to get an answer until, finally, a lady responded on the other end. Remember, these were the pre-mobile days, and landlines to America sounded like you were talking to someone on the moon or using an old ISDN line at an outside broadcast.

"Good afternoon, my name is John McCreedy. I'm an athlete from Northern Ireland and require confirmation of my full scholarship offer and travel details to West Texas State. The contract hasn't arrived, and I am panicking a little. Are you able to tell me what's happening?"

Other than the crackling on the line, you could have heard a pin drop in the hall of our Bangor home where the little grey phone sat. I can recall that phone not just because of its colour but because of how long my mother would speak on it to her friends and how she would answer them. "Bangor 61502", she would state clearly, in a posh Bangor accent, but once she realised it was one of my friends, the accent disappeared, and she would yell up the stairs in her standard pronunciation, "John, there's someone on the phone for you. Get down these stairs now."

James, Jillian, and I used to sit on those stairs and bet on when my mother would finally end a phone call with one of her friends, Joyce. They could talk for hours, and just when you thought the conversation was over, they would go on again for another hour – an hour! She had another friend we called "Auntie Unagh," and those conversations would last for a week! Meanwhile, as I stood trembling in the hall, a US-sounding voice emerged: "John, let me put you through to the track department," which did nothing for my nerves. The phone seemed to ring and ring and ring. I was about to hang up; heaven knows I wanted to, until a lady spoke: "Track and Field, may I help you?"

The moment of truth arrived. I tried to explain why I was calling, but was suddenly interrupted: "I'm so sorry, John. The coach at West Texas is no longer with us, so all track and field events have been cancelled for the rest of this year. Your scholarship has been withdrawn."

Silent.
Speechless.
Stunned.
Sore with pain, I could hardly breathe.

And that was that!

What do you do when the thing you fear most comes upon you? I had long suspected the outcome wouldn't be positive, but this was worse than shocking news. How do you respond when someone pulls the rug from under you and your dreams go up in smoke? How else can you react to the single biggest disappointment of your life? Right then, the bottom fell out of my world.

Could this be happening?

My family thought I'd seen a ghost, and I don't recall even saying goodbye to the lady. I just put the phone down and started to weep. Of course, my parents and siblings embraced and consoled me, but to no avail. Nothing could make me feel better. I was undergoing the darkest day of my life, and the most humiliating!

Despite my tender years, the ignominy of announcing to my family and friends that my scholarship offer had collapsed was tough. The news left me feeling like a failure. Never mind my dream of Southfork disappearing out the window; my American dream had fallen flat. Like poor Sue Ellen's gut-wrenching emotions after discovering another of JR's girlfriends, I was heartbroken. My love affair with America appeared to be over. It took me days, even weeks, to recover, but look at it this way – as McKnight had counselled, at least, for me, the waiting was finally over.

Clarity had come, and staying in Ireland was perhaps meant to be. Maybe places like America weren't for someone like John McCreedy from Bangor, after all! I would have to 'suck it up', accept the worst and get on with things. So, I informed my coach, who reassured me but still called the college in Texas a few choice names. He kindly told my running pals at Striders that I wouldn't be leaving, most of whom were sympathetic and encouraging, although not all. I recall being subject to light ridicule from others with a darker sense of humour. My bags were packed and ready to go. They had abbreviated the words of that well-known John

RUNNING AWAY

Denver song to: "I'm Not leaving on a jet plane."

Northern Ireland isn't a place to live if you are thin-skinned or sensitive, as part of any sports team. Not everyone takes life too seriously. Handing over a matter to providence is often the only road we have left, which is how it turned out for me. That phone call had shattered the silence. I stayed put for now and would have to make peace with that. America wasn't on hold; it appeared well and truly over for me.

Chapter Eight -
"Hey, John, You Don't Know Me"

"John, there's a man from America on the phone for you," shouted Mum. I wasn't in a hurry to answer. Following the West Texas calamity, I was shattered and found it hard to be positive. Still, what if it was West Texas, I thought. What if I've had my scholarship reinstated? What if my nightmare has ended? You see, I am the sort of person who still believes something can happen even when others would have walked away much earlier. I've always been like this, yet I discovered that it's not necessarily a virtue; it can be a flaw. Not moving on from setbacks can paralyse people, me included. But my ongoing desire to go to America was rewarded on this occasion. Before any negative news could break - a minor miracle - a lifeline of lifelines popped out of nowhere due to a stateside phone call I could never, in a million years, have expected. Lifting the phone, I heard an accent I recognised, but not the voice of someone I knew. The call was from America, but the accent was closer to home.

RUNNING AWAY

"Hey John, you don't know me; Roddy Gaynor is my name. I'm from Sligo in the South of Ireland. I'm a junior-year athlete with Pittsburg State University in Kansas, and we heard your scholarship offer in Texas fell through. Is this correct?"

I was floored. Who was Roddy Gaynor, from the South of Ireland? I raced against many guys from the South but didn't know Roddy, even though he was a well-known track specialist in Irish athletics.

After a deep breath, I responded: "Sadly, it is Roddy. How did you hear about my misfortune and situation, and how did you get my number?" "Good question! My coach, Dave Suenram, gave it to me," he replied.

Dave Suenram.

That name would subsequently resound around my world and become legendary to all of us in America. I later discovered that Coach Suenram could track a person down quicker than the FBI if it meant signing them for his track and field teams.

"How did he get my number?" I persisted with Roddy.

"We researched you after we heard your scholarship had fallen through," Roddy answered.

I was stunned. I couldn't take it in until Roddy added. "Here's the thing: Would you be interested in joining our university and the track team at Pittsburg State? I have the contact number for Coach Suenram, and I can tell you he's very keen to talk with you. He is a great guy, and you will love him. He said to tell you if you're interested, he will guide you through things step by step."

"Interested? Are you kidding me, Roddy? I would be most grateful for the opportunity - bring it on."

Of course, Gaynor had unwittingly bailed me out of the most devastating and worrying situations of my young life and from the enormous hole I had dug myself. So, yes, I was both interested and ecstatic! Hailing from the Republic, Roddy may not have resembled the angel of mercy I or my family might have expected, but I viewed him as one. Rather than fate,

I'd call it Divine intervention, yet another one of those hidden helpers showing up just when I needed them. He told me about the university and briefly described Coach Suenram's impressive credentials, and suddenly, my American dream was back on track! A lost cause had somehow been redeemed, even though I knew little about Pittsburg State or its location. Every cloud had, indeed, a silver lining!
Once bitten, I also had the sense to ask what was on the table this time. Forewarned was forearmed!

"Is it a full scholarship on offer, Roddy, and is this a genuine proposal?" "Yes, John!" came his reassuring reply. "Don't panic about anything. As a fellow Irish runner, I promise everything will go smoothly for you, and the coach has also assured me you'll get a contract in the post ASAP." This was reaffirmative beyond re-affirmation.

I was stunned. Opportunities to sign a full athletic scholarship to America rarely come once in a lifetime, let alone twice, and I'd been handed an utterly unforeseen second chance! Perhaps I was destined to get to America after all. That well-worn saying about something being in the stars for you sprang to mind, but was this meant to be, or an even higher power at work guiding my 'New Balance' trainers from Ireland to the USA? And where was Pittsburg, Kansas, anyway? I came off the phone running to look it up, and it was so obscure I couldn't find it initially. I was searching for Pittsburgh, Pennsylvania, but this Pittsburg (ending in a G) was in the heart of the Midwest near Kansas City. Later, I learned that Pittsburg, Kansas, was named after Pittsburgh, Pennsylvania. It was initially called "new Pittsburgh" - a city in Crawford County, located in the South of the state, near the Missouri state border, with a population of over 20,000. Today, it remains the proud home of Pittsburg State University. When I looked it up all those years ago, however, I discovered a smaller college enrolling around 5,000 students.

Today, it enrols approximately 7,400 students, 6000 undergraduates and 1400 graduate students. Founded in 1903 as the Auxiliary Manual Training Normal School, it became a full-fledged four-year institution in 1913 known as Kansas State Teachers College of Pittsburg, or Pittsburg State for short. Over the next four decades, the mission was broadened beyond teacher training. In 1959, to reflect this, the name was changed again to Kansas State College of Pittsburg. Finally, on April 21, 1977, Pittsburg State University was born.

RUNNING AWAY

Today's campus includes the $30 million Kansas Technology Centre, a state-of-the-art technology programme in Kansas's most prominent academic building. In December 2014, the university opened the Bicknell Family Centre for the Arts. The Bicknell Centre provides Pittsburg State University with its first proper performance facility since 1978, when deterioration forced the closure of Carney Hall. In addition to the Linda & Lee Scott Performance Hall, the facility houses a 250-seat theatre, a 2,000-square-foot art gallery, a grand lobby, a reception hall, and a multi-use rehearsal space for large musical groups.

It is no less impressive when it comes to the sports facilities. The $13 million, 154,000-square-foot Robert W Plaster Centre was completed in the Spring of 2015. It includes a 100-yard turf field, an 11,000-square-foot modern strength facility, a 300-metre track and seating for up to 1,500. It also includes locker rooms for men's and women's track & field, football, offices, and meetings.

The facilities at Pitt State are unquestionably hugely impressive today, but even in the 1980's, they were incredibly advanced compared to Ireland. And Suenram's ambition greatly impressed me from day one. For example, when we eventually spoke on the phone, he sounded sincere and much less hysterical than the previous scholarship promoter. His feet were firmly on the ground, and he made no secret that he intended to keep mine there. "John, I can't promise things will be easy for you. You'll be homesick for a while and may have problems settling into a new country, but in time, you'll adjust. Besides, you'll have Roddy from your part of the world to help you, and I will give you every support you require."

That was welcome news and a different tone from West Texas's previous pitch.

Then the clincher.
"I've already steered one athlete to a national cross-country championship victory in 1972, and that's my goal and target for you," Suenram stated casually.

Notwithstanding, my experiences with West Texas State had left me feeling more than a tad cynical. I was nervous about the whole episode, but Roddy Gaynor's perfect timing, followed by his and Dave Suenram's guarantees, consoled me very considerably. Life is often filled with strange twists and turns. Our destiny may not be what we plan for ourselves, but it almost always provides what we require when we are in a tight spot. That was the case here.

Like me, Roddy was from Ireland and seemed very happy in America. He was older than me and promised to look out for me, which he did. Big brother would oversee me from day one; no easy task for him, mind you! Looking back, I wouldn't have had such necessary support in Texas, where I would have been alone. Those profound words from Julie Andrews in the classic movie The Sound of Music seemed appropriate then: "When the Lord closes a door, somewhere he opens a window."

It proved true for this young aspiring runner from Co Down. I was so relieved that a window called Pittsburg State had opened unexpectedly. Yet other questions needed clarification.

How good a college was it?

Would I be offered the same opportunity as West Texas?

How quickly could I salvage the disappointment of not going to Texas? The last question was the most important to me. I didn't want anyone to know the state that I had gotten myself into. To save face, I needed to get away to America and get there fast. I didn't have time to look at the closed door: I needed to jump through the new window of opportunity. Recriminations are often futile in life. Manufacturing a better future is a healthier idea. Roddy answered all my questions and proved good as his word, as did coach Suenram, and I would finally reach the United States within no time.

However, notably, my hero and deliverer had come from the 'South of Ireland,' a place that most of the unionist/Protestant community in Northern Ireland probably knew little about. In those days, many Protestants viewed the South as terra incognita.'Suspicions, misapprehensions and fables about the 'South' and 'the other religion' amongst the unionist cohort were widespread in the North. I still remember hearing ludicrous tales in our community about how the rain came on every time Protestants crossed the border, even though most of these sceptics had never been beyond Banbridge! (Yes! The very same as the famous song 'In Banbridge Town in the County Down.')

Nevertheless, as time progressed, I discovered the exact opposite. The sun appeared each time I crossed the border into 'the South.' It was the North where the rain pelted down. I had run at many Dublin tracks like Santry Stadium and the new Belfield – Dublin's equivalent of the Mary Peters Track - and even competed on the roads and grounds through Dublin's famous Phoenix Park, and the sun always shone there, more than in the North. Even today, Dublin and the South are some of my favourite destinations, and the people are marvellous, but back then, we weren't even allowed to mention the "D word in our community.

It has taken a generation or more to begin to counteract such bigotry and intolerance. People like me became brainwashed into harbouring suspicion and fear of the other religion and the place dubbed "The Free State." Still, thankfully, now I can reject prejudice like this and treat people as I find them, not judge them by their skin colour or religion. While all the problems have not yet been solved, times have changed for the better in Northern Ireland. Sadly, in the Eighties, my parents and their generation became affected by the unsettling events of the Northern Ireland 'Troubles,' yet in many ways, it was understandable. Fear and paranoia stalked the streets of our land, and no one knew what each day would bring or who they could trust, and, so confirming old prejudices for people like my parents.

But following Roddy's bombshell phone call, even my wary mother appeared overjoyed that someone had offered a real and positive alternative for her broken-hearted son, and, at that moment, she didn't seem to care what source or country it came from.

"A man from the 'South of Ireland' has rescued John's scholarship to America," shouted my delirious Mum in the living room.

"God bless him! They should make that man the Pope," my shocked but equally delighted Dad replied.

Now. There was progress!

Blood is always thicker than water.
At that moment, I'm convinced Mum secretly forgave my beloved Bridget

and other Catholic girlfriends, offering three Hail Marys in return!

An incredibly decent guy, Roddy Gaynor was a talented 800-metre specialist who, had a lightning kick and could outsprint most athletes, including me. A three-time All-American at Pitt State, he was well-known and respected in Southern Ireland as one of their best half-mile exponents. A former National Track and Field champion at Dublin's Santry Stadium over 800 metres, Roddy represented Ireland numerous times during the 1980s.

While he had a decorated career at Pittsburg State University, one can only imagine the additional accolades and recognition he would have brought to Pittsburg had he competed his entire collegiate career there. For example, Roddy had spent the first couple of years of his American scholarship experience in Arkansas and, before meeting me, had experience helping freshman students find their way, as detailed in Frank O'Mara's outstanding and inspiring book 'Bend Don't Break' – a record of the Limerick-born man's struggles with Parkinson's before the age of fifty.

This courageous, engaging and uplifting memoir will surely touch every athlete and human being. Notwithstanding, Frank recalls the hilarious story of how, before he left the shores of Ireland for an athletic scholarship in America, his mother insisted he wear a brown wool pin-striped suit to make an excellent first impression. When Roddy, his travelling companion, met him at the airport, he remarked, 'You know how hot it is over there, Frank? You'll fry in that suit.' 'I'll be alright.' Frank insisted; however, like me, Frank would soon learn that Roddy was right. America was definitely not Ireland when it came to the weather!

Although Roddy's time at Pittsburg was short, it was long-lasting for PSU and the track and field programme. Due to his success on the track, in the classroom, and in his local community, doors swung open from Ireland to Pittsburg, Kansas.

In the coming years, five additional Irishmen, myself included, also came to compete for the colours Crimson and Gold. Those athletes combined to bring the All-American honours to Pittsburg from the Emerald Isle to a remarkable 16, along with countless conference and district championships. Pittsburg's extraordinary tradition and record in Track and Field is legendary, but a piece of that legend is the role of the Irish, and one can only say indeed, without fear of contradiction, it would not have proved possible without Roddy Gaynor!

I remember how strong his legs were compared to my skinny frame. When I ventured out in shorts to run around my hometown, I regularly heard someone shout: "I've seen better legs hanging out of a bird's nest." I also avoided running past Bangor's Glenlola Girls' School because if the girls had seen my legs, they would have run a mile, and I didn't want that because I fancied a few of them. When I went for a walk, I used to wear three pairs of trousers to make girls think I was a hunk like the local rugby guys. Boy, was it warm inside those trousers, especially at a nightclub!

In contrast, Roddy was well built and looked more like an Irish out-half than the flying machine he undoubtedly was. He hailed from Sligo, a coastal seaport and County Capital on Connacht's West Coast. Due to its adjacent coastlines and countryside on the Atlantic coast of Ireland and its connections to the famous poet William Butler Yeats, this beautiful town has become a significant tourist destination. In 2023, there were widespread celebrations in Ireland to commemorate the 100th anniversary of W.B. Yeats becoming the first Irishman to win the Nobel Prize for Literature.

Still, growing up, I knew little about Sligo. Ireland had been at war during our youth due to the ongoing 'Troubles', so to my regret and loss, I had never had the opportunity to sightsee in Sligo, even though it was just a hop, skip and jump over the border. With Roddy having been brought up on one side of the border and me on the other in the North, we never let the differences that had separated our societies ruin our relationship, even though many American citizens seemed obsessed with getting us talking about 'The Troubles' and the separation it had caused. Roddy and I always believed that what we had in common as Irishmen more than outweighed any division between our communities and our people.

We were sports people first and foremost. We also learned that in America, everyone appeared to have a cousin from Cork or a friend from Fermanagh and regularly became fascinated about 'The Troubles' and how I managed to 'dodge the bombs!'
Explaining the problems about our homeland in America wasn't easy. The

faith that you were born into in Ireland generally shaped your politics. Catholics were deeply attached to the country's reunification, while most of the Protestant community preferred remaining within the UK. Times have changed, however, some Catholics are happy enough to live within the UK, while some Protestants are fed up with Britain, Brexit and failed politics, leaving them much more open to the real possibilities for a new Ireland of the future. The situation in Northern Ireland is complex, yet it is not so. Back then, however, things were at boiling point at home, and here I was, being given the chance to escape the deep divisions within my country. How could I turn down such an invitation?

I was keen to take Roddy up on the offer to join Pitt State as soon as possible, so I wasted no time following up by accepting the offer from Coach Suenram, someone who would shape my thinking and life just as my previous mentor and coach, Tony McKnight, had done before him here at home. It was almost like Dave Suenram was waiting in the wings, destined to take over the work Tony had started. Following Roddy's timely intervention, Coach Suenram's appearance birthed another hidden helper in my life at the perfect time. Not that Tony and he were alike. They were completely different individuals.

Dave Suenram was a much stricter kettle of fish and had a more demanding personality than my previous coach. He also proved reliable and good as his word, producing my four-year athletic scholarship offer within days, not weeks, and arranging to collect me at Joplin Regional Airport in Missouri. The fact that I would be gone from my Bangor home and life in Ireland within no time at the end of August 1980 was proof, indeed, of his serious intent and remarkable organisational ability.

In the end, that wasn't so surprising. If Dave Suenram wanted someone on his team, he would stand on his head to get them. He personified a winner and was just the man I needed to get me to the next step of my promising athletic career. But thanks to a guy from County Sligo, whom I'd never previously met, my American dream was back on track. And no one, besides my family and coach, had any idea of the torturous road of travel it had taken to get me there. The old adage is true, and, if I may paraphrase, fate is often stranger than fiction!

Chapter Nine –
Leaving Loch Lao – Saying Goodbye

One final phone call was all I required to secure my path to the United States, a call I certainly wasn't expecting. Billy Elliott, a local athletics enthusiast, had watched me develop at North Down AC long before I joined Annadale Striders. He had observed my progress through the junior ranks. He would often take me in his car to race, even though I had long since moved from North Down AC. After winning the Northern Ireland Junior Cross Country Championships in Lurgan, Billy was one of the first people to congratulate me.

When some of my fellow athletes from Bangor remained a little bruised at my joining Annadale, Billy stayed a friend. He encouraged me and reminded me that I represented our town of Bangor, no matter which club I ran for. I loved his approach to life. Then, after hearing about my good fortune, he went a stage further. This excellent unseen hand phoned our home to offer to pay for my return airfare to America. That act of kindness still resonates deeply with me, even to this day, and was most certainly part of a providential plan regarding my scholarship at Pittsburg.

RUNNING AWAY

Little did he know, I had been saving like crazy for my flight with part-time jobs where I had a paper round at a local newsagent called Pollocks and worked at a well-known chemist's called Balmer's on Bangor's Main Street, but I was still way short of the airline ticket price. The paper shop was famous in the town, as reliable as the church bells at Bangor Parish. A little white metal bin with a fading Dale Farm ice cream logo sat outside. The lady who owned the shop was incredibly dedicated. A famous story goes about how a young girl was sent to the shop late at night by her grandmother protesting: '"It's bound to be closed by now," only to be told by her Gran: "Don't worry, she would stay open if she thought 10p was coming up the street." I always found the lady grand, but you wouldn't return with a pound short from your round, that's for certain – and I made sure I didn't!

On the other hand, Balmer's felt like a promotion. I worked as a storeman sorting out the medicines for collection, even though I had smugly informed most people I was 'a pharmacist.' I had an eye for a lady who worked in the shop called Avril. She had bright blonde hair and beautiful dark eyes. She was a lot older than me, but was good-looking, elegant, and kind to me.

Notwithstanding, what a white coat and folder can do to a person at 18 years old is remarkable, especially as they walk down the main street promoting it under their arm. In those days, I walked around Bangor like Frank Abagnale Jr., played by Leonardo DiCaprio in the film 'Catch Me if You Can,' genuinely convinced I was Doctor Conners. I was only responsible for stacking box after medical box in the storeroom and delivering prescriptions, but I was living the dream as a doctor.

Bumping into a friend at the lights at the top of Main Street, I would be asked: "What are you doing with yourself these days, John?"

"I'm in medicine," came my reply.

It wasn't untrue. Remember, I took McKnight's honey recipe three times daily! Having trained twice that day and lifted heavy boxes at Balmer's, no one needed to rock me to sleep at night.

Eventually, however, I gave up both jobs before heading for America. Finally ready to depart my beloved homeland, I recall an uneasy silence in our kitchen at teatime, apart from the uncomfortable sound of rattling plates, cutlery, and cups. That kitchen dining table – the scene of our last supper together – overlooked our long, narrow back garden near Park Avenue and brought back emotional memories from my childhood and youth. I had been stung in that garden by wasps and bees, got badly burned on a sun lounger, and managed to destroy virtually every plant or flower using the grass to play football. I had even witnessed my mother catching my dad puffing at the garden fence after he had vowed to give up cigarettes.

What gave my father away that night was the massive trail of smoke above his head, not to mention the stench from his clothes as he returned to the house, continuing to protest his innocence. Then there was the sight of our next-door neighbours' broken garage windows, which James, I, and our pals had been mainly responsible for breaking on more than one occasion with a ball during penalty kick competitions. The entire street would turn up for a pre-match kickabout before the English FA Cup final each year, and sadly, the Sloans, our next-door neighbours, paid the price. They used to fix the windows yearly, but I think, dear love them, they eventually gave up.

"What will you do when you get to…you know…?" my tearful sister, Jillian, whispered, refusing to use the 'A' word.

"I've no idea, but it will never be home, Jillian," came my disingenuous reply.

The truth was, I couldn't wait to board the plane. I was sick of the Northern Ireland conflict, of division and bigotry, and tired of the seemingly endless cycle of violence. I longed to travel and see the world. Imagine, arrival in a new country would mean no more having to walk into premises and raise my hands to be searched, no more being evacuated from shops and buildings, and worrying about being shot dead or caught in the wrong place at the wrong time! No more fear of a bomb exploding indiscriminately. No more bitterness, bias, or strife. For the first time in my life, I could take people as I found them, not look into their eyes, concerned about what religion they happened to be. If I were a paranoid and slightly damaged teenager, I consoled myself, but the ongoing unrest hadn't helped. I needed to get away from it all and go somewhere more normal.

RUNNING AWAY

For me, America couldn't come quickly enough.

"So, you're leaving us here to fight it out," came James's cynical contribution a reference to those ongoing 'Troubles' and how I had become one of the few fortunate enough to escape the chaos we all constantly had to endure. I couldn't disagree with James, even though he seemed to display a flair for sarcastic wit at precisely the wrong time. In many ways, this was not an uncommon reaction 'across the divide', as it were, in Northern Ireland at the time.

"True, but you guys will be okay!" I replied, unsure they would be, of course. It was a worrying time, leaving them in what was, at times, perilously close to civil war while I escaped to the States. I wasn't sure when I would return to Ireland, nor were they.

Like always, I was first down for tea. My sister, Jillian, a picky eater, had no interest in food; her white pimply face and skinny frame often told their own story. Our Dad was constantly concerned about Jillian's weight. 'Eat up, you pasty-faced ghost,' he would scold her. He always had a great turn of phrase, my Dad. He saw it as 'tough love' with Jillian's best interests at heart. But she needn't have worried about leaving any food on her plate; a constantly famished athlete, I was always on hand to help! James was frequently slow to get to the table, but wouldn't come up for air once there. Our mother had spoiled all three of us: Jillian, her little favourite, and James, who would even point to where he wanted his gravy. I believe I was her No. 1, or so she told me. I think she played the three of us off against each other. I regularly thought nothing of eating Mum's meal, too.
"Go on; I see you are looking at it," Mum would say as I ogled her plate full of meat and mash, even though my own helping was long gone.

"No, mum, you need to eat too", I replied hypocritically, hoping my mother would kindly pass me her food. What a contrast to my dad, who showed great control in leaving his beef until the rest of his plate was cleared. Every night, he would start with his potatoes, then work through the vegetables and finally polish off the chicken, beef, or fish on his plate. I sat him out on many occasions to see if I could pick up some of the scraps, but he ignored my plaintive hints and finished everything himself.

"For goodness' sake, give the boy something; can't you see he's hungry?"

protested Mum, but my dad insisted he taught me a valuable lesson about never assuming anything. His father, my grandfather McCreedy, was the same. He would never let me win when teaching me to play draughts. My granny would scold him every Sunday, but he wouldn't give in until I learned to beat him fairly.

"Let the wee boy win, you cruel man," shouted my granny.

"No, I won't let him win until he wins alone," answered my Grandad.

After this, I hardly lost a game of draughts. Well done, Grandad McCreedy! Sometimes, tough love is the best form of love. Looking back, I was blessed growing up and came from a loving and caring family. My parents had forfeited so much to get me to where I was. Dad was a good worker and provider, while Mum sacrificed the last part of her dinner many nights when there wasn't enough food for her three children. A growing boy and a constantly hungry athlete back then, it would have been easier to keep my photograph. So, as regards food, I welcomed my sister's and mother's love and any leftovers during those days.

I still remember the doorbell ringing as we sat in the kitchen that night. Mum thought it was "wee Davy," picking me up to train at 'the Mary P', then remembered that her son's summer training at the track was over, and it was the night before I departed for a new life abroad. No more beautiful, scenic daily runs along the famous South Belfast Lagan Towpath or through Bangor's Ward and Castle Parks. Instead, I was America-bound. I was excited but also apprehensive. The caller turned out to be a friend with an important message: "The newsagent says they've some outstanding money for you, and you've got to come and get it before you leave."

"Are you sure the money is for me?" I spoke. "Yes, of course.' replied my friend. "Happy days, then; I didn't think I was due anything else,' I confessed.

Upon hearing of my good fortune, I threw on my coat and sprinted out the door. I remember skipping down Castle Street, cutting through Market Street, and racing down Dufferin Avenue to the shop. I had always felt butterflies approaching that shop, but no more. On this occasion, I was collecting money, not bringing it. It would be the final time I would go there. 30 pounds was waiting, which wasn't a fortune, but I still felt rich and lucky.

Wisely, our goodbyes were said at the front door of our central Bangor home. Except for my brother James, who drove me to Aldergrove (Belfast International Airport) in his bright yellow Capri. His first car was his pride and joy. He would race it around Bangor's Seacliff Road every Sunday night with his fellow band members, Mark Crockard, Mark Armstrong and Marty McConnell, in what was known as the "Whacky Races" until some bright spark came up with the idea of speed bumps which put an end to the 'Bangor International Grand Prix!'

Even today, motorists must crawl along Seacliff Road, but at least the view is breathtaking. Maybe that was the whole point! People rarely stop to observe creation anymore, but you get plenty of time in a car on Seacliff Road. James thought the world of that Capri until I brought him back to earth, insisting he drop me short of the airport entrance in case anyone saw us.

He was insulted, but the sheer noise from the exhaust alone drew everyone's attention while hefty thumps sounded from the vehicle from our hometown of Bangor, something James had assured me was normal. The suspension was so low that the car would have passed as a yellow submarine rather than a yellow Capri. I'd been forced to sit in the back, which had nothing to do with being chauffeured or trying to make me feel like a celebrity athlete on his way to the big time. The front seat was exclusively for his girlfriend, Carolyn. No one sat in that seat except her. Come to think of it, nobody got near the bathroom when Carolyn stayed at our house. I am not suggesting he was obsessive, but when Carolyn was in there, James used to sit outside the door guarding it like a stiff-backed sentry until the coast was clear.

My departure to America proved a significant moment for James and me, given it was the first time we'd been separated since meeting in our mother's womb. Unusually for twins, I was a full hour older than James, giving me the "big brother" status. Few believed we were twins as my "wee brother" was nearly five inches taller than me. I teased him that I was better-looking, though! Now, as we confronted separation for the first time, he would have to fend for himself. As children and young adults, we shared prams, clothes, and food and went to school together.

But I played various tricks on him and occasionally let him know who was the boss. James got his own back for many of those misdemeanours years later – and how!

Neck and neck in a local cross-country race, and knowing I was fitter and might sprint ahead in the closing stages, he cleverly explained that we were twins. He subtly reminded me we had shared countless things in life, recalling stories of when we wore the same jumpers and shorts, sang together in the church choir, and sat beside each other in school. I couldn't argue how close we were, and I remember feeling quite emotional. "Let's hold our hands up and run into the finish line together as twins do?" he suggested.

"What a NOT so lovely idea," I thought to myself! I was the current Northern Ireland junior cross-country champion and used to winning races, so initially, the proposition didn't grab me. Sharing first place or losing a local race in my hometown would be unthinkable!

If I were going to win, I would win all by myself! Notwithstanding, I agreed to the truce because, unknown to James, I'd always felt slightly guilty about how my little brother had been somewhat overlooked for facilitating my running ambitions. Here was my chance to finally repay him with genuine kindness.

"Let's wait until we are a little closer to the line before joining hands", James added.

Our good friend Robert Lyle was in third place and closing. It was risky slowing down like that, but naively, I again agreed.

Then came a moment that, all these years later, still stings and fills me with resentment. Just yards from the tape and taking me completely off guard, my beloved twin took off and raised his hands in victory, leaving me in second place. I wasn't livid; I wasn't even angry; I just felt sick! How could he do such a thing? I had an athletic reputation to protect. I could have choked him right there and then! I would never speak to him again, unquestionably.

"Sorry about that, Bro; I couldn't resist it," came my brother's pathetic excuse as he tried unsuccessfully to hug me and make me feel better.

RUNNING AWAY

"You have to admit, it was coming!" he added.

At that moment, I needed to draw on all those early church sermons about love, forgiveness, and self control. It didn't work. I was fuming. I found words within me that I didn't realise existed. When I arrived home and told my parents what my scheming brother had done, I assumed I would find sympathy, but instead, they were in stitches, which incensed me more. I think they knew I was good value for it, too. Poor wee James had finally stood up to me, and they loved it! All those 'liberated' apples and various little tricks I played on him during childhood returned to haunt me, and I deserved every bit of my comeuppance. Eventually, we made up; oddly, I even came to respect him for his actions.

However, sibling rivalry like that meant little to me when I arrived at the airport. We both knew it was time to enter different worlds and experience separation for the first time. We didn't always share the same interests; yet only twins understood their special bond. It was an emotional moment, but, being grown-up lads, we didn't cry tears in front of each other, only after we had parted.

While I wasn't running away from my friends and family, the opportunity to head to America was too good to miss. So, thanks to Roddy, Dave, and Billy, the latter having kindly agreed to cover my airfare, my American dream soon became a reality, and the big sweat was over. True to his word, Billy Elliott bought my tickets, and I was finally leaving on a jet plane for America, not knowing when I'd be back again. I had never been further than Scotland, Paris and the Isle of Man! I had just turned nineteen, and suddenly, the world was at my feet!

Many further-educated friends were headed for colleges in England, Scotland, and Wales, but here I was, about to jet off to the Great Plains of America. Could this be happening to me? Innocently, I probably took all this support and voluntary assistance from those early encouragers for granted because I had no idea just how timely and effective they were. Yet without them, I wouldn't have gone anywhere. It may have been 'No' to Texas, but it was still 'Yes' to America, and from this point on, for me, there would be no looking back.

Chapter Ten - "Welcome to America, John!"

A novice in air travel, by 1980, the only thing I knew about frequent flying was a sprint session at the Mary Peters Track or firing a paper aeroplane into the bin.

Nevertheless, having said goodbye to James, I cleared security, dried my eyes, and was London-bound to catch a connecting flight, unaware of the drama in store.

I had been on many boats - even pleading with my mother to "let me off" one as it sailed to Liverpool on a choppy night at age five - but not planes - and never on my own. Arriving at St. Louis airport, I resembled the hapless Victor Navorski (played by Tom Hanks in The Terminal, someone entirely out of his comfort zone and unsettling everyone around him.)

I wasn't scheduled to reach my destination of Joplin in the southwestern corner of Missouri until the evening. Oddly enough, I had turned down a leading university in Missouri but somehow ended up in the Missouri region. I was just relieved; I was finally in America. I even asked myself, "How did I end up here?" But I had. Clueless, perhaps, but it was me, alright. The sun was scorching during the day, but whistling wind and torrential rain appeared by nightfall, giving me an early glimpse of Kansas's volatile and quickly changing climate. Summers there are hot, often sweltering, and generally less humid, and winters are highly changeable between warm and very cold. However, I was in for a huge culture shock in America, not just about the weather conditions.

RUNNING AWAY

Initially, I would suffer from an identity crisis where I would feel alone, even though most Americans I met were extremely friendly and hospitable and made me feel welcome. I soon discovered that the issue wasn't with my newfound countrymen and women, it was brought about by typical student homesickness and the introduction to a strange environment I was clearly unprepared for. As I said, Americans were incredibly welcoming and even concerned for my welfare. The words of Coach Suenram before I left Ireland would come to pass. I was missing home. Nonetheless, in those days, seeing cars being driven on the opposite side of the road to what I was used to was quite a novelty and not the only observation I made early on.

After arrival on American soil, I was instantly struck by the number of black people travelling through the airport in St. Louis. In the 1980s, Northern Ireland had few foreigners or people of colour. I only recall one black person at our school who disappeared as fast as he arrived, especially after he announced that he followed Scottish Football giants, Celtic! I had hardly spoken to a black person in my youth, so this was something new, and my initial conversation didn't go too well. Leaving the airport terminal door behind me for a stroll outside, I felt a wall of warm air like nothing I'd contended with before. It was over one hundred degrees on the day of my arrival. Once those doors opened, my face broke out into a heavy sweat, which quickly had me turning around and walking back inside. "How am I going to run in conditions like this?" was my first thought.

Contemplating whether to go outside again, I was harassed and jostled as busy commuters knocked me over and growled at me for blocking the doorway. Like the neurotic Navorski in The Terminal, I gripped my luggage tightly and took another run-up to give me the confidence to try again. America was open; all I had to do was walk through those doors! I was still petrified at what lay behind them, but it was too late to return to Ireland. For me, it was sink or swim time!

Holding a brand-new suitcase and training bag – yes, I had finally ditched the white sewing machine; I moved outside as the doors swung open, only to face that intense heat again. Trying to make sense of the extreme conditions, I began to console myself that the hot air was coming from somewhere other than the US climate because nowhere could be this hot. There was a strong, hot breeze, which felt like air-conditioning in reverse. Then I spotted an African American lady sitting on the ground, presumably waiting for a bus or a taxi, so I decided to be friendly and talk with her.

"Excuse me, ma'am, where's all the warm air coming from?" I asked.
I know, what a question!

Let's reread it: "Excuse me, ma'am, where's all the warm air coming from?"

To this day, it haunts me. I still can't believe I uttered those words, but I did.

The lady glanced up, looking at me like I'd escaped an asylum. "Say what, man!" she responded.

The old saying goes, 'If you're in a hole, stop diggin', ' but not me. Oh no, I carried on regardless. I was determined to get some answers, so I persisted.

"I've just arrived from Ireland, and I'm wondering where all the warm air is coming from?"

I'm not defending myself, but we didn't live in the era of information and technology to the same extent as today, nor was flying as popular as it is now. There was no such thing as Sat Nav or Google Maps. Many young students travel the world today and are familiar with the temperatures of many countries, but really, I had hardly been out of Baltic Bangor. I knew where America was, but hadn't experienced the living environmental conditions. Before this point, my idea of a holiday was a trip to the North Coast of Ireland, where it would blow the head off you even on a summer's day. Okay, I was still naïve, but this heat was something else! Eventually, the lady stared at me incredulously and laughed aloud before bellowing, "That's the heat, man, that's the heat."

Her lit-up eyes were accompanied by her head shaking.

"Did you say you were from Ireland? I think you've come from outer space, man," she added.

RUNNING AWAY

Today, there's a lot of talk about aliens, but they were around in 1980 – yours truly being one!

Red-faced, I hurried back inside and regrouped. I wasn't a teenage student travelling alone; I was now officially an international embarrassment, unfit to be let out.

By evening, when I arrived at Joplin Regional Airport, the conditions had changed. Jack Suenram, son of the head coach, Dave Suenram, picked me up there. Although used to pouring rain at home, I'd never experienced a worse rainstorm than when Jack and I took the short drive to Pittsburg, Kansas. It was so bad that Jack could hardly see through the window, and the fading light didn't help us. I was scared and convinced we would have an accident, especially when Jack overtook other vehicles at speed. Being relative strangers, we didn't speak much for most of the journey, making things worse.

As I sat nervously, trying to reassure myself that all was well, I recalled some dark movies I had watched involving serial killers who pick people up at airport terminals. You know, the sort where the same people never reach their intended destination, and the car detours through a dark forest for sinister reasons. What if Jack wasn't who he said he was? Maybe I was being kidnapped? Wearing a little peek cap and glasses and appearing socially awkward, he could have passed for anybody. All sorts of absurd thoughts went through my head. I was out of my depth and hadn't even arrived at my destination until, ultimately, my fears were unfounded.

Jack was a great guy and helped me considerably during my American adventure. More importantly, he safely drove us to my new accommodation in Pittsburg, Kansas (with a G). Mind you, this small but wonderfully welcoming city caused my mother no end of problems once I set foot in America. When she met people in Bangor and told them her son was at university in Pittsburg, Kansas, they often replied, "You mean Pittsburgh, Pennsylvania?" 'No, I mean Pittsburg, Kansas,' she would answer. "' Oh, you must be mistaken, Winnie; Pittsburgh is in Pennsylvania."

"Yes, it is, but my son is at Pittsburg, Kansas – it's Pittsburg with a G! I know where my son is, thank you!"

That was my mother all over.

As I said, Mum always loved having the last word and putting people right—and she was right about this one!

Exasperated, she used to wail, "Do they think I don't know where my son is situated?"

That first night, my new surroundings were dark, and with very few streetlights near the house, I had a knot in my stomach as we entered the driveway. I'd initially hoped to be housed in the residence halls, following the short drive of around 25 miles from Joplin to the campus. Instead, I ended up in a small wooden house that was quite a walk from the famous Garfield Weede Gymnasium, where I would spend most of my time representing the team known as The Gorillas. Garfield Weede was an American Football, basketball, track and field coach, athletic director, and one of the first college coaches to "break the colour line" and allow racial integration among his players. I was privileged to share the house with Coach Suenram's son, Jack, a skilled racquetball player and presumably someone assigned by the coach to look out for me at that stage.
Poor fellow!

Like Roddy Gaynor, he didn't know what he was letting himself in for!

As was common in Kansas, the rainstorm had passed by the following morning, and a sense of quiet was restored. It felt stiflingly hot and uncomfortable. I recall an unpleasant and distinctive smell from the damp conditions I had not previously experienced at home. I assumed it was from the heat, but on reflection, it may have been cannabis! Leaving the house for the Weede Gym at around 6:30 a.m., I was filled with excitement and no shortage of trepidation. It was my first day at college in a new country, and I knew no one, but I was thrilled and enthusiastic. Although Coach Suenram had yet to introduce himself to me, I got an early indication of the kind of person he was from the house's residents directly beside us, which appeared to be occupied by several black athletic students. One of them, Darryl, who would become famous amongst us at Pitt State, was a top-class sprinter with a unique gift for running and for welcoming international students like me to the campus.

RUNNING AWAY

As the front door banged behind me, I jumped off the high porch onto the street, where I spotted Darryl and his party pals. Their hats draped over their faces; you knew they weren't sleeping. Without glancing up, Darryl suddenly remarked: "John Boy's going to run," a statement that caught me off guard as I passed the door. The others remained motionless, too, responding, "That's cool, man, that's cool."

I was shocked! I wondered how they all knew my name and who I was, having not yet been introduced to a single soul, but, as I would discover, word travelled fast in Pittsburg. It was a small town, and everyone seemed to know everything and everyone. They'd been expecting me and wanted to introduce me to traditional college banter. As I later learned, I was quite a catch for the region, coming from Ireland. Then, just as I thought I was in the clear, Darryl shouted what seemed like a warning to me, "Coach is going to whip his butt." The rest high-fived and agreed, 'Yeah, man, the coach will kick his ass."

What sort of welcome was this to the USA? Yet a more important question was: What sort of man is this coach, Suenram? I had heard that he was a nice guy. Instead, Darryl and his colleagues had painted a picture of a trainer rubbing his hands in glee at the thought of running me ragged—something that wouldn't be too far off the mark, as it turned out.

Coach' kicked my butt numerous times in America, but that was his job! That said, he was also kind, helpful, and interested in my welfare, not just how I competed on the track, but he remained incredibly focused and didn't suffer fools gladly. He would run the legs off us to get the best out of the team. Whether you came from Pittsburg, Boston, Baltimore, Baton Rouge, or Belfast, his training sessions could be brutal. In the immortal words of Tony McKnight, my coach back home, if you survived those sessions, you were an athlete, not a jogger.

Walking to the gym that next morning in August, I passed the beautiful college grounds and the halls of residence where I had assumed I would be staying, and my eyes lit up when I saw the outdoor sports stadium with an impressive track and American football pitch. Someone had beautifully cut the lawn beside the library, which looked quite stately. When I entered the Weede, I couldn't believe an indoor track and basketball arena also existed. Talk about luxury! The sky was the limit for me. I had arrived in America as a rising athletics star, but the sporting priority at colleges in the States would soon humble me. American football was out in front regarding celebrity status, followed by basketball, while way back in third was Track and Field Athletics. If I were to make an impact in Pittsburg, I would have to do something spectacular. As I set off for that first morning's training run with the guys, naturally, I was desperate to do just that and impress the coach. Instead, I was about to receive a valuable cultural lesson - never underestimate the Kansas climate.

It was a Thursday morning, and I knew it was hot but didn't realise it was over one hundred degrees. During the first mile of our ten-mile run, the team crawled along, which almost drove me insane. Some had barely warmed up and seemed to be limping rather than running. I could smell alcohol, and they appeared exceptionally unfit and probably were. It was the start of the new season, and the night before hadn't helped. Every Wednesday evening was 'drink and drown" at their local.' It was three bucks for all you could drink. Referred to as 'The Training Table,' it wasn't the best spot for track athletes with a rigid training session the following day.

No wonder our teammate Dan Hinton claimed he didn't want to be there. As he pulled his vest on each day before training, I remember Hinton would sigh, then remark with little enthusiasm, "We've got to do this stuff all over again." He weaved from side to side like a learner driver instead of running ahead, which meant he would bump you off the road if you ran next to him. At first, I was convinced he didn't like me, given how many times he elbowed me off the pavement. No one had ever shoved me off the road like that before! That first morning, he must have elbowed me a hundred times until I could take no more. In no mood to hang around, I had come to Pittsburg to impress, and here was my first opportunity. I had finished the track season in pretty good shape at home and couldn't stand the pedestrian pace.

We knew we'd run a mile in Pittsburg when we reached the end of the roads because many were marked as one mile long. Reaching the mile mark always felt like an eternity and an achievement, especially on warm days. Those roads were hot and prolonged, leaving your legs feeling crushed.

Making it to the end of them was a marathon all by itself. Sometimes, all we could see was a mirage in the distance. After about a mile and a half of dull pace and Hinton's elbowing, I decided to kick on at my usual training speed. Ignorance plus arrogance are fatal, especially in an unacclimatised young person from a foreign country. Unfortunately, I possessed both characteristics in abundance. I soon opened a considerable gap on the rest of the team and felt proud of myself as I passed Coach Suenram's truck at the five-mile point, still feeling relatively fresh. I was streets ahead of the rest of the team, even the older, more experienced athletes, and I was waving like Steve Ovett sprinting down the home straight in an Olympic final.

"That should impress the coach on my first day," I thought.
"Just be careful, John; it's hot out here this morning," he counselled in his slow midwestern brogue. His wry smile told me I was running too fast and headed for trouble.

"I'm fine, coach, trust me," I replied.

"Okay, but you'll learn," he added.

And how?

I was used to putting in a shift in training back in Ireland, so I ignored him and kept going at the same pace until, around seven miles, I hit what's known in athletics as "The Wall." It usually happens to marathon runners, but it can happen to anyone in extreme heat, especially those not acclimatised. Suddenly, I began to feel exceptionally weak and sick and, to my shock-horror, was reduced to a jogging pace as my legs completely seized up and became like jelly. I had never experienced a shutdown like that before. To make matters worse, it wasn't long before I heard the footsteps of the chasing pack closing on me, my fellow athletes, and someone who would become an exceptional friend to me in the States – Scott Currier. Like Roddy Gaynor, Scotty was a few years older than me and possessed a fabulous sense of humour. He was a guy who could party hard and run fast with no apparent aftereffects.

Like Coach Suenram, Scotty called a spade a spade but knew how to look out for his friends and teammates. He was a genuine team player who came from a stable and loving home, and it showed. In my case, he proved a brother born for adversity on more than one occasion.

Looking back, I wouldn't have survived my American experiences without him. But his sense of humour could be cruel, too. As the group finally caught up with me, they couldn't have failed to notice my distress due to the extreme temperatures, but they breezed by, seemingly uninterested. I half expected them to say something encouraging like "Keep going, John" or "You can do it, friend." Instead, no one made a sound except Scott, who waited before whispering: "Welcome to America, John."

I saw the rest of the team sniggering as they ran on, leaving me feeling quite foolish, but I had deserved my large slice of humble pie. I was in America now, not Ireland, and I needed to learn that. I would soon respect the weather conditions in Kansas or die. Even being manhandled off the road by Hinto was preferable to how I felt at the finish of that first ill-fated training session. I've always regretted not tucking in beside him and staying where I was.

I didn't recover that morning, trailing in at the back of the group with no shortage of egg on my face. My trainers were wet and smelling at the finish; I could have wrung them out. It caused Currier to place a warning sign on my locker to the rest of the team, which read: "Enter at your own risk" – a sign that remained for the rest of my days in America. But those embarrassing moments at the airport, the cultural blunders with the track guys, and the humbling experiences on the Kansas roads were all part of my freshman induction programme. They were necessary to adapt well and begin to do what I came to do – break records and win races. I also learned something important, namely that, in America, warm air was, er, exactly that – warm air!

Very warm!

So, I had no choice but to follow the old proverb, "When in Rome," and I gladiatorially did.

L-R: Myself, Lyle and Roddy.

Chapter Eleven –
Does Anyone Know Where Ireland Is?

Autumn proved a beautiful time in Pittsburg, Kansas. I still remember it like it was yesterday. The sun shone, and the campus, as always, was immaculate. Despite the falling leaves, the grass held up and looked almost greener than in Ireland. I'm walking to training, carrying my little sports bag on my shoulder, a bag I have had my whole life: my training shoes, towels, stopwatch, and track kit.

I could see Darryl approaching following an early morning sprint session. With his hand in the air, he zoomed in on me like a swooping bird. It frightened me, and I thought he was going to attack me, so I walked past with my head down. I had done this to Darryl several mornings before Scott eventually mentioned it to me.

"Darryl thinks you've got a problem with him, John. Do you not like him?" he questioned as we gathered for training.

"I don't dislike him, but I am suspicious of him," came my reply.
"Why suspicious? What's the problem?" said Scott.
"He walks towards me, rocking back and forth with his hand held high, looking like he's on glue. I jump out of his way in case he thumps me.

It's not that I don't like him. I'm convinced he doesn't like me," I responded.
With that, Scott and the rest of the team were in hysterics.

"Listen up, Kid, he just wants you to give him FIVE."
"FIVE What!" I responded.

"Give him an American high-five by slapping his hand, and he will be on his way. He wants to say Hi, that's all," Scott responded.

Was it really that simple?

Physical expression has always been a lens through which to view a culture, and this was another essential part of my social development and societal insight into the United States. Once I knew what Darryl wanted, it would be rude not to 'high-five' him.

So, I reached out to my fellow American athlete the very next day. As he approached in the same manner, this time, I was ready. As he swayed towards me, I jumped in the air and whacked his hand as hard as I could, which had him burling around and shouting, "That's it, man, that's it. You've got it now!" His unrestrained joy was evident.

I knew nothing about that part of American culture, but after that, I loved nothing more than my campus showdowns with Darryl. He would block me at every turn until I gave him that firm hand of friendship.

I would slap Darryl as I passed by and heard him say, "Way to go, man." In a few seconds, this talented runner had made my day and enriched me.

But I had come to America to run, and as I approached the gym, I was excited at the thought of another day of training under Coach Suenram's watchful eye.

Despite previous accomplishments, Suenram retained a burning ambition to produce a solid team and another NAIA national cross-country champion, even though he had created one previously. In the era of Jim Ryun, Steve Prefontaine, Frank Shorter, and many other top American distance runners, Suenram had already coached Mike Nixon to national championship glory in 1972 but appeared determined to see another of his stable become the number one athlete. So, imagine how great it made me feel when following my embarrassing debut training run in extreme heat; he still considered me a potential National Cross Country Champion, especially if I made good progress under his carefully planned coaching. I was super excited, and who wouldn't have been?

All training sessions were geared towards this significant National Championship event in November, and no one seemed more obsessed with it than Coach Suenram. That meet was all he kept reminding us about. Other races came and went, but he didn't seem to care as much about them as what he described as "The Big One".

In training, no quarter was asked or given as we completed 'fartlek' sessions in the local park, sprint sessions on the track, and murderous mileage on the roads. I hadn't yet turned twenty but was running around 100 miles per week. I wasn't built like some other athletes, so my skinny legs were taking quite a battering, but my progress was visible, and I was excited.

I could feel myself improving – the reason I'd come to America, so I didn't argue at that stage with the punishing training programme. Once, as we completed a 20-mile time trial, the coach told me that if I had kept going at the same pace, I would have crossed the line in under 2 hours and 20 minutes for a marathon. That was scary yet also thrilling for later in my career.

But such optimism was masking a more significant problem that I was experiencing – chronic pain in my calf muscles. Many athletes had hamstrings, knees, or Achilles injuries, but mine was in my calves. I had always felt this pain, even before I left for America, and I had always endured it. Once there, however, it increased and developed into a terrible trial. The pain became quite unbearable, but I was dedicated and determined in those days and wisely or unwisely continued to run through the pain barrier. I hadn't come this far to quit. I would have put up with anything.

Some days, the discomfort was worse than others, but I became more conscious that I was making remarkable progress by running through the pain barrier. Suenram had asked me several times to be careful.

I was bent on success in those days and ignored his caution. I had no idea how serious the injury was, so naturally, I kept running. I finished well in several races in the Fall, yet rarely without some pain. I won several races and remembered finishing runner up in a top college cross country event before the nationals. Suenram couldn't wait to tell me afterwards that I was on course to win a national championship one day, although he knew it wouldn't be that season.

Pain or not, I continued to train at high intensity. Hindsight is a wonderful thing. Had I known the damage I was doing to my frail frame, I probably would have cut back on the mileage I was clocking up and concentrated more on my speedwork. I had no idea then that the punishing schedule I was following would come back to haunt me so severely. I was improving, and what wasn't to like? However, those performances to date did not indicate what I could and would ultimately produce at the NAIA Championships that same year. If I could break into the top forty in my first year, I would have three more years to win the title.

Suenram had very high standards and expectations from his athletes. He insisted on maximum effort and discipline from his runners but had a generous side, too. He would rarely compliment you, so you knew you had done something right when he did. He called a spade a spade and ensured you knew where you stood. He commanded respect and loved seeing his athletes getting faster, stronger, and better. What more could a young athlete ask for from a coach?

We all dreaded the last quarter of any training session with Coach Suenram. It was always the hardest, especially when surrounded by guys on the track quicker than me. No one looked forward to the last quarter when Dave Suenram was in charge. There was no mercy. I knew I wasn't coming home first if I hadn't shaken off the likes of our 800-metre specialist, Roddy Gaynor and our best miler, Johnny Johnson. They should have been behind me at that stage, but sometimes they weren't. Both had a better kick than the rest of us.

Like McKnight back in Belfast, Suenram would be hollering like a maniac if we were late around the turns, while the back straight in the park felt like hell itself. When it came to preparation, Currier was a martinet who refused to be beaten, even in training. He used to leave his guts spewed out on the ground. I hated yet loved training with him because he pushed me to new levels, but killed me getting there. We all cursed and swore and called coach names under our breaths, but he knew this. Pushed on by others like Dan Hinton, Steve Ortiz, Robert Marquart, Lile Budden, Robert Skeen, Jeff Stein, Bob Olivia and many other track guys, it felt like we were racing each other every day, and in truth, we were.

Russ Jewett, who also competed for Suenram and was eventually appointed as coach of the PSU team, is on record as saying: "Everyone who knew Dave Suenram, especially anyone he coached, has a 'Coach Suenram story.'"

It was true, and I was no exception, even in 1980. My favourite memory of Coach was watching his eyes gazing at the stopwatch. It was a focus I had never seen before. It was passion, pride, and belief all rolled into one. I recall how athletes ran past him, causing the coach to contort and shout, "Pick it up." His face was in agony. All he could see was the clock. Even when we were on time, he still wasn't satisfied. He reminded me of our old Civil Service mantra on timekeeping: "If you're on time, you're already ten minutes late."

He always wanted more and never settled for anything less, which probably explains why Pitt State had such an excellent pedigree in track and field. If ever a man prepared his team meticulously for the national championships, it was Dave Suenram. Coach Suenram maintained a tremendous pedigree throughout his career, serving as the men's cross-country coach at PSU for 21 seasons and guiding Pitt State to seven conference titles.

During that time, he worked 19 seasons as a men's track & field coach (1968-86), leading the Gorillas to seven league titles in eight years between 1979-86. His track & field teams placed in the top 10 five times at the NAIA National Championships, highlighted by a fifth-place team finish in 1985 and sixth-place showings in 1983 and 1986, and he coached nine athletes to national championship performances in track & field. Suenram's cross-country teams also scored in the top 10 national finishes in 1975, 1977, and 1980. But more than all his accomplishments, Suenram was a first-class individual and a lovely man.

Finally, the 'Big one' arrived, and we were ready and chomping at the bit. I can still recall the warm winter winds and light breeze before the start of the November National Championships. It was November 15, 1980, like a spring day in Ireland. It was the day Suenram and all of us had been waiting for – a day, however, that almost didn't happen for me. Those calf muscles began to play up badly during the previous week, and I could hardly walk, let alone run. I would face some of the top athletes in American universities, so a crippling injury was all I needed.

Aside from the World Junior Cross Country Championships, this was probably the best field I had ever had the chance to compete against, and yet here I was, limping around before the race had even started. Coach Suenram knew I was in pain, so he had a plan. Before the start, the coach gave me some painkillers, which remarkably did the trick and helped me to race unhindered, although to say I paid for it later is no exaggeration. Boy, did I ever! If I couldn't walk before the start, you should have seen me limping onto the bus later that day.

"Don't let me down, guys", Suenram drooled before the gun in that trademark mid-western brogue. "This is the biggest race of your lives, and all eyes will be on you today."

The weather was unusually mild and sunny as I posed in my Pitt State kit for a photograph before the start. That picture captured me with suntanned legs in November, so I sent it home to my family, and it ended up in our local paper, The County Down Spectator. The Spectator carried reports of my progress in America, including those national championships. Imagine me with suntanned legs in November! For once, those white, skinny sticks looked quite decent. The event turned out to be memorable for several reasons. Pitt State scored a top-ten national finish, and Scott Currier and I finished in the top 30. He was six places ahead of me in the twentieth position. I was delighted for Scott, a fearless runner who gave everything in training and racing. It was his best performance of the season. He epitomised courage, guts, and a never-say-die spirit, but he had talent, too. He exceeded all expectations that day, leaving some more highly fancied athletes in his wake due to his determination. However, afterwards, he'd privately joked that it was fear of Coach Suenram that had him running out of his skin! I knew what he meant.

"I had no alternative but to run my butt off," claimed Scotty.

The race was won that year by Pat Porter from Adams State, an athlete who became a seasoned U.S. distance runner and two-time Olympian, running the 10,000 metres at the 1984 and 1988 Olympics. From Minnesota, Porter graduated from Adams State in 1982 with a degree in marketing, after which he became one of the most dominant U.S. distance runners of the 1980s. Having scooped three national NAIA crowns, Porter ran eight World Cross Country Championships during the 1980s, finishing as high as fourth in 1984. From 1982 to 1989, Porter also managed to do what no American had ever done: win eight straight USA Cross Country Championships. At those nationals in Salina in 1980, we were, of course, unaware of who Porter was or that he would go on to become such a successful athlete.

Fittingly, Porter was inducted into the Rocky Mountain Athletic Conference Hall of Fame in Colorado Springs and placed into the Adams State Athletics Hall of Fame in 2000 in Alamosa, Colorado. He became quite a hero of mine, not just because he had obvious talent, but mainly due to his dogged determination to consistently outrun his opponents.

Meanwhile, at Salina, I was just a second behind Kearney State's Shane Fruit, a young athlete who left a memorable impression on me that day, not just in an athletic capacity. Despite a colossal effort, digging in with everything I had, I couldn't catch him for the last quarter of the race and couldn't work out why. Without pain, I flew as fast as I remember running in any race I had ever run. It was such a relief not to feel aching legs. I was at my peak fitness and was flying in the last quarter, but I still crossed the line inches behind him. I should have been pleased, even delighted, with my performance, but I felt gutted at being unable to reel him in! Then, to my astonishment, he turned around and embraced me, repeating, "Praise the Lord, brother." Those words came like a bolt of conviction at a religious rally and through the mouth of a man I had never met and didn't know.

"Praise the Lord, brother?" Who says that directly after a running race? Yet he certainly seemed to have some form of Divine assistance because, try as I did, I couldn't catch him. Even now, I remember those words and their lasting impact on me. I even wonder how much they played a role in my spiritual development in my late twenties.

People who come to faith often have a 'lightbulb moment' or a memorable turning point. I am no exception. My opponent had planted a seed within me, which watered and increased with time, but not immediately. Matters of the soul are a strange thing. Some people seem to have a damascene experience, like Saul, who became Paul, the apostle in the New Testament book of Acts. Others take time to embrace a new path. I was in the latter category. Spiritual issues were not my priority back then.

My journey and agenda weren't just about running. I had come to America to succeed in life. The world was my oyster, and, as I saw it, I had bigger fish to fry! Back then, I felt like I could do what I wanted and go where I wanted, but life would eventually teach me otherwise. Pride would come before many a fall.

Nevertheless, those 1980 NAIA Championships became memorable not just for our team's success, where we finished in ninth place. Looking back, I had finished in the top positions in the national championships, raced against a future Olympian and American superstar, Pat Porter and experienced a moment of divine inspiration all in one day! I even got a suntan in November. Not a bad day's work now!

I hadn't expected to win the race, but given my injury problems, I was happy with the result. I was concentrating on my running, studying and life ambitions, and things were going according to plan. And, when it came to learning, there was no shortage of humour on offer. During that first year of my P.E. degree, I signed up for various subjects, including biology and American Government, which became an eye-opening and, at times, comical experience. For example, I was introduced to the American Government class as "John from Ireland." The lecturer asked me to stand up before announcing, "Does anyone know where Ireland is?"

It took an eternity for a young man to rise to his feet, put his hand in the air, and call out, "Sir, isn't that somewhere near Switzerland?" It still makes me smile.

As part of those academic commitments, I was regularly scheduled to study at Pitt State's impressive library on a weeknight. It boasted what was considered the prettiest and cleanest small lawn in America. However, I can't recall completing too much of this activity, nor can Coach Suenram or anyone else at Pitt State. Scott used to follow me and lead me back to the library. I'm convinced Suenram had assigned him to shepherd me. While I loved sitting outside on that beautifully cut lawn with books in front of me, making it look like I was interested, try getting me through the library doors. I had no desire to go there regularly.

"Have you been going to the library, John?" Coach Suenram asked occasionally.

"I sure have, coach", I would reply falsely with slight American intonation to settle him, but I don't think Coach was taken in. He knew exactly where I was and what I was doing, and it had nothing to do with my coursework. I was just as often in the sports games room, playing Pacman, to be precise, a game that had become a dreadful distraction and preoccupation. The 1980 computer game Pacman was probably the equivalent of Supraland or Windjammers. I'd never been into video games per se and never have been since, but for some reason, for that brief period, I became passionate about this one. It became an obsession. The problem was that I needed a quarter to play it, and I went through my weekly allowance quickly. I would play until I reached my last quarter! It left me with quite a dilemma. Would I spend it on one final shot at glory or keep it for something more essential?

My allowance from a part-time job at the Weede Gym had already been spent trying to outwit the little gremlins as I attempted desperately not to be killed off. Once, when I was down to my very last quarter, I had to make the painful choice between making my weekly phone call home to Ireland to my family or trying to become a computer wars champion once again. To my shame, I kept the quarter, chose Pacman, won, and had to wait for the next airmail to arrive from home.

Those next weeks were dreadful, pacing up and down, waiting for the postman, especially when he walked by the house each day and didn't deliver anything. It reminded me of my West Texas fiasco! Only then did I realise how costly the decision to win at Pacman proved. I gained quite a reputation for playing Pacman, which was concerning, considering I had people investing in my athletic potential. I wasn't there to be a Pacman star, but a track star! What was I doing? Yet, as my colleagues were about to discover, I had already graduated with first-class honours in another discipline, and the USA was the best place in the world to study it.

Chapter Twelve -
A Horse Between Two Mattresses

In the 1980s, America wasn't just the land of the free and the brave but also a nation full of exciting food. It was hard to deny the warm, fuzzy feeling of biting into an American burger that most people had been enjoying during the 1970's and the 1980's. The boom of fast-food chains then made America famous for more than its movies. The stranglehold of McDonald's, Burger King, Pizza Hut, and other giants of the Eighties ensured competition was stiff. However, the United States is more than a Fast, junk or processed food haven.

Many citizens there possess an impressive appetite for good food, which I took full advantage of. Come to think of it, there was no better person to sample endless culinary creativity due to the numerous and unexpected invitations I received to American homes, and all because I came from Ireland. It seemed like everyone wanted to make me their favourite adopted son, and I heartedly embraced this welcome and surprising kindness. I felt like an American President visiting Ireland. Everyone wanted to shake my hand, and I felt like a celebrity. I hadn't achieved anything remarkable, but I was from Ireland, and that was all I needed to ensure my ticket to numerous American banquets.

"Guess who's coming to dinner?" the locals would say to their friends. "The young Irish guy on the track team." For them, it was all about learning more about the Troubles and Ireland. For me, embarrassingly so at the time, it became almost solely about the food.

The problem was that they might as well invite over the entire American football team that same day. I was not a light eater in those days, and we didn't do "small portions" where I came from. Mum was mainly responsible for this. She said I was the only person who had to have three plates of chips with a salad. "You won't die if you don't eat a bag of potatoes daily," she told me, but she kept serving them. Ultimately, my reputation for food spread to America, where scores of hidden hands queued up to fill my seemingly insatiable appetite, which suited me just fine. After all, I needed all the carbs I could get. Following the training, I could have eaten a horse between two mattresses.

I'll never forget my first eating excursion on the American dining scene. It came when Coach Suenram and his delightful wife, Norma Jean, invited me for dinner – a day I still remember. It was stiflingly hot, but we completed an entire training session despite the intense heat. The offer to eat somewhere else that day, other than our campus house, was, to be honest, too good to be true. I was tired of Jack's and my leftovers. I hadn't experienced the luxury of a home-cooked meal since I had arrived, and the thought of a proper dinner – one like Mum used to make - brought great relief. Mum was a magnificent cook and should have opened a restaurant. She would have made a fortune. I've never understood why she didn't.

Indeed, I never appreciated her cooking more than when slumming it with Jack in that house in Pittsburg. On this day, after finishing training, I was parched, more than starving. Thirst is one thing, but feeling blisters in your mouth is another, which is often how we ended a training session on a hot Autumn Day. I headed to the Suenram's and immediately spotted a glass of what I assumed was cold Coca-Cola. Naturally, I gulped it before spitting it all over the table. What an entrance, and what had I just downed! It was arguably the most disgusting drink I'd ever tasted. Of course, I was ashamed of my behaviour and apologised profusely until the coach asked, "What's wrong, John? Don't you like iced tea? I thought you would be familiar with it in England?"

Suddenly, it all made sense.

"I'm not from England, coach. I'm from Ireland, and we like our tea hot, piping hot, not cold like that!" I replied. I had never heard of iced tea then, and even though I tried to like it after that, it wasn't for me. So, I never drank it again, while cola has never tasted so good despite its high sugar content. Even the sight of iced coffee now gives me the shivers and reminds me of that embarrassing arrival at my coach's home.

When the meal arrived, however, it was an altogether different experience from the drinks menu. It was awesome! I don't think I've ever tasted better fried chicken, mashed potatoes, and sweet corn! A guilty pleasure, if ever there was one, is sizzling American Fried Chicken, which was born to go with mashed potatoes and sweet corn and was always my favourite dish, even in Ireland, where fish and chips and a good steak, along with fresh fish and homemade stew were the constant traditional competitors. But I had hit the jackpot in America regarding classy chicken!

Historically, while fried chicken and chips have always been associated with America, Scottish immigrants were credited with bringing the deep-fried method across the pond, something that was soon capitalised on by Colonel Saunders, who spotted a commercial opportunity in the 1930s and started pressure-frying breaded chicken in his secret spices at a service station in Corbin, Kentucky; thus paving the way for none other than Kentucky Fried Chicken and, of course, all the other fried chickens which soon followed, like nuggets, fingers, popcorn, and patties. Even today, Pittsburg is well known for being the epicentre of 'the chicken wars' between 'Chicken Marys' and 'Chicken Annies' – two delicious fried chicken restaurants situated side-by-side.

I was already familiar with the town's fast-food outlets like Kentucky Fried Chicken, having worked for the chain in my hometown of Bangor before I left for the States. It was another one of those part-time jobs I found to help fund my trip. It was situated at the bottom of the town's Main Street, and I remember quickly becoming one of the primary servers, which had its perks. Everyone who came into the shop wanted a breast of chicken. When we got down to the last few pieces on an evening shift, I would scrape up the remaining parts with chips, box them up and put them somewhere safe to take them home to my family, who naturally couldn't wait for me to return from work. They had always made me feel welcome, but I was treated like a king on those nights. James and Jillian would meet me at the door. With concerned faces, they would ask, "Did you get it?" They weren't talking about the Watergate files but five pieces of succulent chicken and chips. That said, no matter how good Kentucky was, Norma Jean's fried chicken remains, for me, the best in history, even though a wrong choice of drink almost ruined it and left me feeling utterly embarrassed. Thankfully, that night didn't put a stop to my wonderful invitations to dinner in Pittsburg. Another invitation came almost immediately, but that occasion proved much more problematic. The night turned sour for me when the lady of the house announced that the dish she had cooked was laced with what she lauded as 'delicious red onions.'

Now, there were only two vegetables in this world I couldn't eat – onions and turnips. My mother spent sixteen years serving me turnip, and I left it on the plate for sixteen years. Then, one night, after a row because I wouldn't eat it, my laid-back father finally stepped in. Unusually, he raised his voice and scolded, "John doesn't like turnip. Never serve it to him again." And Mum didn't. I was proud of my dad, but wondered why it took him so long to intervene on my behalf.

Growing up, however, I detested onions more than turnips, so I didn't know what to do as I was keen to impress the couple. In our teens, my twin brother, James, used to arrive home reeking of onions at all hours, having eaten at a seafront fast-food joint called Charlie's Burgers. I was not too fond of that place, but he loved it.

The couple, the Morrisons, were from the adjoining county to me. They hailed from Larne, a ferry port in County Antrim – just north of Belfast - and had come to Pittsburg on a teaching exchange with their daughter. When they heard of my arrival, they kindly offered a hand of hospitality to one of their fellow countrymen. Northern Ireland folk are like that. Naturally friendly and hospitable.

"How long have you been in America, John?" I was asked.

"Just a few months," came my nervous reply.

"Do you like onions?" the lady asked.

My stomach began to turn.

"I have made lasagne with lots of onions; how does that sound?" continued Mrs Morrison. They were such a beautiful couple, full of kindness and encouragement. At 19 years old, I had no experience or courage to tell them the truth – I hated onions and wasn't having them! What a dilemma! The lady had stood all day preparing her dish, and I didn't wish to offend her. The smell of those onions alone was making me feel sick. Lasagne without onions is delicious, but this combination was lethal!

I remained tight-lipped until Mrs Morrison noticed I had hardly started mine after serving the meal. She said, "Eat up, John, or your food will go cold." Finally, as the well-meaning couple disappeared to the kitchen for drinks, a lightbulb moment arrived. I grabbed my athletics training bag and swept the entire plate of food into it. When they emerged from the kitchen and saw my plate empty, I expected her to congratulate me, lift it away and offer me some dessert, but instead, she filled it to the brim again, much to my dismay. I would have been delighted to receive another full plate on any other night, but this was one occasion when I couldn't stomach it anymore. "I heard you liked your food, John, and are a big eater, so we have made two pots for you. You started slowly, but that first demolition was impressive by anyone's standards, wasn't it, Alan?"

Her husband nodded in approval while I squirmed in my seat.

"We've been told you always need at least two or three portions, John," said Alan. "The track guys say they have never seen anyone with such an appetite," he added.

Of course, I made flimsy excuses about being full-up, which had never happened before, and left early to do some revision - code for a visit to McDonald's on the way home. Those burgers and fries hit the spot that night, for sure! Meanwhile, the poor Morrisons had been so hospitable, but they chose the wrong ingredients that night for me. Come to think of it, I spent weeks getting the smell and the onions from my trainers and clothes while the bag went in the bin. If Scott thought my locker stunk before 'Onion-Gate,' that locker smelled like a decomposed body after that. He even called a company that evicts rats and mice to fumigate the place, but it didn't work.

But it wasn't my last visit to the Morrison's House. Roddy and I were invited several times after that, and they made my night when, after dinner, Dallas hit the screen, and we all sat down and watched the latest episode.

Those encounters aside, I reserved my most notable eating performances for my fellow athletes and coaches. When it came to one of those "all you can eat" promotions, the track team and I would usually begin eating early on a Saturday morning at Otto's Café or Harry's Café in the centre of Pittsburg – the latter a delightful little diner that served the most fantastic food. This beautiful and popular restaurant provided the most amazing bacon, hash browns, pancakes, and maple syrup I'd ever tasted. I loved having breakfast there, but it was somewhat curtailed as we weren't permitted to overeat before a big event. The coach could regularly be heard calling up the table, "Only one slice of bacon and toast, John."

My reputation preceded me!

Nevertheless, I had two meals—one on the table for the coach to see and one below, thanks to Scott, who regularly slid extra portions under the table for me.

A true friend indeed!

Thankfully, there was no limit to how much we could eat on our return journey following race day, and this is where I came into my own. The saying "All you can Eat" had never been so true.

Earlier in the year, I had been dubbed by Scott with the nickname "Kid Natural" due to my sporting ability, including soccer and racket sports. The nickname stuck and was eventually shortened to 'Kid, ' which was highly appropriate as I was the team's freshman. The guys used to love watching me juggle a football without letting it slip, and despite having packed soccer in, I could keep the ball off the ground for ages, leaving them enthralled. Scott called it "Kid's 100 Juggles."

Soccer was only emerging in America back then, but many Americans had already heard of the incredible skills of Belfast's George Best. Who hadn't heard of the former Manchester United legend, one of the greatest footballers the world had ever seen? However, after excelling at a McDonald's following the national championships, I suddenly acquired a new nickname that would also stick, but not as flattering. From there on, I became known as "The Bin." It is a term of endearment, yet I could quickly have taken offence.

Each morsel of this gastronomic journey was unexpectedly outstanding, from excellent food to ordinary. Any track athlete unable to finish their portion passed it up to yours truly, and it always found a home. I gratefully accepted everything I was offered with no sense of over-indulgence. Once, when the track team was invited to a college function, which included several VIPs, I was first up for seconds from the delicious carvery.
"Were you not embarrassed, going up like that, Kid?" asked Scott as we left the event.

"Embarrassed about what?" I replied. On mature reflection, I may have changed my response.

In general, America became a case of 'all-you-can-eat.' There were some legendary late-night excursions to Taco Bell, where I spat everything out on my first visit but ended up loving the stuff, unlike the iced tea. Nothing was off-limits, especially at Taco Bell, which served Mexican-inspired foods, including tacos, burritos, quesadillas, and nachos. I was also introduced to the standard American hot dog on our nights out to American football and baseball. Nothing complements a baseball or football game quite like a hot dog. Many fellow athletes seemed to think adding ketchup to an adequately cooked Dog was uncivilised, but not me; I lashed it on. It was the onions that I found uncivilised!

Since July 1916 in the U.S., the international hot dog eating contest has been held, with one winner downing 62 hot dogs in a 10-minute binge. I've always wondered if that's where Scott and the guys got the awful idea to enrol me on a similar college stuffing contest. Over time, my eating reputation had become legendary around the campus, but it made no difference to my physique. I ran the weight off as quickly as I gained it in those days, but I'm reminded of a story about how too much food can ruin a training session.

RUNNING AWAY

Coach Suenram had left a note on the board to say he would be away for one day, and in his absence, the track team decided to go to Otto's for an "all you could eat" session instead of training. After downing everything on the menu, including dessert, the team were shocked to hear that Coach hadn't left the city after all, instead calling training for 2 pm the same day. Naturally, none of the track guys could tell him what they had done, so they turned up in their training gear to try and perform the regular programme. Several athletes became sick, while others couldn't move. The justification given to Coach Suenram was "food poisoning," which was partially true, but thankfully, he accepted it.

The question remained: Who would my competitor be in the big "Food Fight at Midnight" clash, one of the most anticipated duals of the season—and it had nothing to do with sport? Who could match my, by now, legendary capacity for food? An Irish champion at downing fish and chips, burgers and fries, cottage pie, and vegetables, I feared no one.
In the end, we didn't have to look too far. Jack, my roommate and a considerably taller man than I but just as lean and hungry, had competed with me unofficially each night at the house for months. Food-wise, we were a match made in heaven. It was often a case of who could down the most after our separate training sessions – mine running and his playing racquetball. Now we would have the opportunity to face each other in a genuine competitive eating competition.

"When it comes to food, you don't want to mess with me," Jack threatened me as we sparred before the big night.

I would laugh and respond: "Ask my mother, Jack, about the five plates of Cottage Pie I used to put away before going for a five-mile run. You are only a novice, my friend."

He would look at me disbelievingly, but I knew he was secretly worried. Jack and I were extraordinarily fit but were outrageously hungry most of the time. And so, a much grander stage awaited us both than our front living room at that campus house - the evening lights and sparkle of the famous Broadway. It was a long stretch through the centre of Pittsburg and included some of the best-known American food chains. As word spread about the showdown on Broadway between Pitt State's freshman runner and its more experienced racquetball star, many students got on board. Posters were placed everywhere for what was billed as "Food

Fight at Midnight."

When the time came, we were raring to go. Jack and I fasted for most of that day, which was some achievement for us two scavengers. The contest began like an evening out at a heavyweight boxing contest.

"From the United States, we present to you the American eating machine, the undefeated, unbending, and untameable, Jaaaaaaaaaack Racquetball Suuuuuuuuenram," announced the MC, adding:

"And from the Emerald Isle, the diminutive, unstoppable freshman athlete, the man who was invented for fries, we give you Greeeeeeedy, 'The Bin' McCreeeeeeeeeedy!"

Making our way down Broadway from burger joints to fish and chip shops, Taco Bell, and pizza places, the first to evacuate would be the loser. I know. What a sport! But we were stubborn competitors, determined to be King of the Kansas Fast-Food joints, so no quarter was given or taken.

"Jack, Jack, Jack", roared his supporters, while my track mates shouted, "Way to go, Bin!"

We competed ferociously for the first half of Broadway, but after taking in a fish and chip shop, which didn't taste like fish and chips at home, I hit a rough patch. My stomach began to churn, but like a marathon runner who goes through a bad patch at 19 miles before recovering 4 miles later, I soon bounced back and remember downing a burrito at Taco Bell with ease. Eye contact was everything—the first to flinch lost. When neither of us refused to give in, the duel was eventually declared a draw, just in time. The pair of us sprinted to the bathroom as soon as the result was announced, and the rest is history. It was an absurd night, and how I ran a step the next day is still beyond me. I had experienced a drinking hangover several times, but never a food hangover. It was altogether new territory and equally unforgettable.

Chapter Thirteen – Partygate and Pizzagate 1980

The term 'Partygate' sends shivers down my spine, but it has nothing to do with the 2020 shenanigans in London. Words like COVID, lawbreaking, Lockdowns, Boris, or Westminster don't unsettle me; words like Pizza Hut, Police, Coach, and Graveyards do. You see, long before Party-gate 2020, there was Pizza-gate 1980!

Don't get me wrong; I have nothing against Pizza or the police. The coach was fantastic, and graveyards are… well… graveyards. But when you've almost collided through the front window of a Pizza Hut restaurant in a stranger's car in a foreign land, leading to a 'who done it' search for the culprits following a stakeout in the town cemetery, you're not likely to forget such an incident, even 40 plus years later.
Oh yes, that was me.

Detached from all reality, I was unaware we'd nearly crashed through the front window of one of America's biggest food franchises.

At the time, Pizza Hut, which began in Wichita, Kansas, was still relatively unheard of outside of America. Following intense growth, O.Gene Bicknell joined the Pizza Hut franchise network and opened his first Pizza Hut in, of all places, Pittsburg, Kansas. Suddenly, our little city had the bragging rights!

RUNNING AWAY

It was a small city, viewed even by Americans as 'obscure', but we had Pizza Hut, and many others didn't! We felt like the Bethlehem of the Midwest, chosen for greatness, at least when it came to Pizza. I'm not saying Pittsburg was small-scale, but at one of my first parties there, I still recall being shocked when a female student asked me, "I hear you are from Ireland; how did you find us?"

How did I find the front door of Pizza Hut in an American car?

Getting pizza wasn't like today, accessible on every street corner. Back then, it was a luxury in Ireland, even in America, and certainly for me. But what happened next would put me off the pepperoni-flavoured stuff for life. Remember, I was in America to run, and I did, especially the night of Pizzagate. I ran faster that night than I'd ever run on a track. Looking back, I'm convinced I may have broken 4 minutes for the mile that evening, but I've never been able to prove it.

Things had started routinely enough. We'd gone to a house party, not imagining for a moment how reckless and ridiculous the night would end. The party was like any athletic student house revelry in America in those days – entirely out of control. While Pittsburg State University competed admirably with other colleges in track and field, basketball and American Football and was proud of its sporting and business heritage, it was also second to none regarding partying. This aspect of American 'culture' opened my eyes to life in general. I wasn't streetwise, despite 'The Troubles' in Northern Ireland. I'd grown up sheltered in the town of Bangor due to my focus on athletics and the 'curfews' at home after dark. Staying out late in Ireland meant returning by about 7.00 pm. So, I didn't experience many house parties and proper wild nights until I reached America.

The university's 'great and good' were at this rave. I felt in the 'not so great' category. Besides feeling quite nervous, I was the only sober person there. I was a disciplined athlete! And there's only so much Coke you can drink at a party. Besides, I found it educational to observe my fellow athletes and others go from being learned and cultured individuals to being wildly inebriated. I was also amongst some butch American football players with women drooling over them. How the other half live! My light physique did not match them. I could only offer, apparently, a cute accent!

John McCreedy

My partner in crime that evening, who shall remain nameless (that's between me and my Maker), became increasingly intoxicated, eventually banging a snooker cue against the wall, almost taking people's heads off, mine included. Threatened with brain damage, I knew it was time to get him and me out of there, but we had a sizable difficulty. We had arrived in his car, and he was in no fit state to drive anywhere, let alone take me home. He fought ferociously with me to get into the car, but I refused to let him. We argued the toss on the street outside for some time, almost coming to blows, before I suggested driving it myself, a bold move for someone who had never driven an automatic car, let alone driven on the right side of the road.

Some help, I was going to be!

But I was sober, and he wasn't. I hadn't a clue how to drive an automatic, but I was up for giving it a go—anything to stop my boozed-up companion from killing us both. Leastways, I'd always secretly dreamed of driving one of those impressive American gas-guzzlers, even if, ultimately, it would be me who would almost kill us and others in one of the most bizarre incidents of my life. Figuring out how to drive the automatic took me a while. Slumped in the front seat, my intoxicated friend had passed out and was now in the arms of Morpheus, and of no help whatsoever. We chugged and stopped, staggered and started.

I recall getting out several times, pushing the car, and asking people for assistance, but most passers-by had been at the same party and were in no great shape to answer or cooperate. Then, I managed to get the hang of it briefly; momentarily, everything seemed better. So, I threw caution to the wind and pulled out onto Broadway, the main street in Pittsburg. It was the most audacious decision I had ever taken, even more dangerous than defying Mum to continue my relationship with Bridget. I should have been petrified with an empty road in front, no license, no clue of what I was doing, and a passed-out passenger beside me; instead, it was the opposite. I was suddenly in seventh heaven. From Bangor's relatively quiet byways to Broadway's bright lights, I was an international student steering a sizeable American car down the Super Highway!

I felt like John Travolta in 'Grease' or Paul Michael Glaser and David Soul in 'Starsky and Hutch' cruising down the boulevard before a major raid.

RUNNING AWAY

I'd grown up watching the American detective show and always fancied myself as a cop, but my lack of height would end all such notions. I even became cocky, picking up the speed until I realised I didn't know where the brake was, as we unsurprisingly careered off the road hurtling towards Pittsburg's famous Pizza Hut. Racing toward the front window, for the first time, I could relate to how the captain of the Titanic must have felt as the doomed luxury liner headed straight for the iceberg. Carnage seemed inevitable and imminent, no matter what I did. Of course, I tried desperately to shift the car away from the window, but couldn't manage it! I didn't have enough time; time to figure anything out!

I had to find that brake and find it fast; otherwise, my scholarship, athletic career, and perhaps even the lives of others would be over. At that moment, my whole youth seemed to pass in front of me. I saw an orange jumpsuit, hard labour in an American prison and occasional letters arriving in my cell from home. I imagined myself sweeping the streets, unlike at home, where inmates have a TV and a personal gym and can order Chinese from their cell at the weekend. Then, miraculously, with seconds left, I stopped the car straight in front of the window or below it. To this day, I'll never know how, but we survived. Just centimetres away from the window. Lovers had been enjoying intimacy and a late-night pizza until a clueless driver from the Emerald Isle and his inebriated co-passenger disrupted their serenity in the most sudden and surreal way.

I hope no one had chosen to propose at Pizza Hut that night! It would have been disastrous. Of course, the customers just stared out the window in wild disbelief and horror. Why wouldn't they? Looking back, I must have prayed a million prayers in those awful, possibly life-changing, indeed life-threatening final seconds before we rudely interrupted their harmony. I'm convinced every prayer was answered.

Meanwhile, my friend was still out for the count on the passenger seat beside me, having missed everything. There are none so blind as those who are liquored up! I took a deep breath and collected my thoughts. The car may not have ploughed through the restaurant's front window, and I had no alcohol in my system, but my final resting place was far from standard parking in Pittsburg. The car was jammed almost beside the window. I had an intoxicated companion, no permit, nowhere to hide and no idea who to call. People from the restaurant ran out to see if we were

okay, but it was them I felt concerned about. I tried calming them down by telling them everything was normal.
"Relax, folks, stuff happens," I said, acting cool.

"Don't panic; it's no problem!" I added – as if ramming a car underneath a restaurant window was a frequent Friday night 'evenement'.

Can you imagine young Americans back then saying: "Hey, let's go out and shove a car through a restaurant window tonight?"

"Let's do it. That sounds like a great idea!"

Making the situation even more ludicrous and bizarre, I asked: "Is there any pizza left?"

Okay, so it was a poor attempt at humour, making it look like we'd dropped in for a late-night nosh, which, of course, we had, unconventionally!

Years later, I remember taking a flight from Bucharest to Rome, the worst and scariest flight I've ever been on. The thunder and lightning were so ominous that we tried to land thrice and aborted each time. When the pilot finally got the plane on the ground and came through the airport terminal with his crew, he rightly received loud applause from the relieved, grateful passengers, to which he humbly responded, "It's all in a day's work."

Meanwhile, I had averted my version of a near disaster on the ground, where no one was injured, but I became public enemy number one. Then, following the outraged diners' dirty looks and aggressive comments, I had an idea. A colleague once told me that if you are involved in an accident, just run for your life and explain later. Yeah. Right!

But it wasn't long before I got to test his theory, mainly when the siren of a police car could be heard in the distance. To this day, I don't know if it was heading for Pizza Hut because I took off, taking my boozy partner with me, which was no mean feat! Most of the way, I had to haul my friend as he couldn't stand up until we reached the local graveyard – the darkest part of the journey.

RUNNING AWAY

Even though we'd got offside relatively quickly, the car remained stuck, jammed tight to the restaurant. We had belted for the nearest street and just kept going. We seemed to run and run and then walk for miles until tiredness and exhaustion set in. I was shattered. It was late, and we were freezing. How had it come to this? It was the middle of the night, and I was in a cemetery with a lifeless college friend and with a huge problem on my hands - a grave situation if ever there was one! (Or was it a deadly dilemma!?)

As we collapsed under the stars, my pal slept, and I lay thinking. I knew I needed to return to Pizza Hut, apologise, and confess, but it was too dangerous. I recall how pleasing the stars were that night. Peaceful and orderly, perfect in the sky - a million miles away from my current chaotic circumstances. Strangely, I had always imagined lying underneath the stars someday with the girl of my dreams in a foreign country, reluctant to leave that place. Instead, I was cuddling up to a blitzed male college student whose snoring was unbearable. Yet bizarre as it may seem, taking comfort beneath those stars proved the ideal location following the pizza-gate incident because it gave me time to reflect, regroup and take stock of where we were.

I reasoned that if God created the universe and made the stars as beautiful as they were in the sky that night, I could be quickly delivered from this extraordinary mess if I prayed hard enough. I knew it was a big ask, but what other choice did I have? I was now caught between a rock and a hard place. I needed all the help I could get. There were no mobiles in those days, and no YouTube, WhatsApp, or TikTok on-the-spot videos. Who would know any better if I quietly removed myself from the chaos? No one would be any the wiser if I left my unruly pal in the graveyard and fled home. Alone!

After all, it was his car and his problem! Just leave him to explain, and the dilemma is solved, right? Then, another idea struck me. I would call Coach Suenram. I had his number. I would call him and tell him what a hero I'd been. The story would go like this: I spotted a drunk athlete and offered to give him a ride home in his car, only to misplace it opposite the front wall of a local restaurant. I would say that I gently rolled the car up to the window and parked it. That should work. I could use the excuse that I had not yet learned to drive on the right side of the road and had never driven an automatic, but that my motives were clearly noble.

Yeah, right! The coach wouldn't buy any of it. Like Tony McKnight before him, he hated the idea of his athletes wasting their money and time on parties, drinks, and horseplay. As that dreadful night wore on, we fell asleep, woke up near dawn, and went home separately. I was dreading the morning, even though the morning had come. It was around 6 am. I approached our little wooden house, feeling tremendous relief as I jumped onto my porch to go to bed until that man, Darryl, greeted me with words that shook me.

"Hey, John Boy, that was a close shave, my man."

Like always, he'd been pretending to sleep again on his balcony but was wide awake. I don't know how he used to perform so well on the track! "What do you mean, a close shave, Darryl?" I replied nervously.

"Man, you nearly bumped your head on the doorpost there," he replied.
I breathed another sigh of relief, pleased he wasn't referring to the accident earlier. Who knew about this incident? It was indeed only a matter of time before word spread. Pittsburg was like any other small town; tongues wagged, and people talked. It was too public to hide. I was in deep trouble. I got no sleep that morning, eventually crawling out of bed to the news that I was to attend a meeting at the college campus later that day. I, of course, assumed the worst. It was probably game over regarding my scholarship and career. I had regrets—more than a few. I had done it my way, and now it was payday. I formed letters to send to my parents, coach, and anyone else who might still speak to me. How could I explain being sent home? Mum would be fuming.

Back home, in luminous contrast, my local paper had just reported on how well I was doing in their sports section, noting some of my more impressive athletic performances since arriving in the States. However, had they picked up on this story, it would have been front-page, not back-page news. The Spectator would have loved a headline like: "Bangor Athlete in Car Crash Caper" The story would have raised a few eyebrows, too: Nineteen-year-old Bangor athlete John McCreedy, on scholarship in America, found a unique way to enter the front door of Pizza Hut in Pittsburg, Kansas, recently – in a car he didn't own or couldn't even drive!! What a scoop for the local boy reporter.

I wrote a million lines in my head, but in the end, it didn't matter. Mercifully,

RUNNING AWAY

I didn't require any of them!

Remarkably, we were both given a fool's pardon in a stunning change of fortune, and the subject was closed. The powers that be seemed to write it off as "youthful horseplay" by "two idiots," which probably summed up the night and was about right. I didn't require any of those apologies, which I had prepared. Instead, my nameless friend and I were surprisingly free to go. The relief was palpable, and we didn't hang around to ask why, either.

I remember feeling immense relief, but wasn't totally off the hook. The coach would get us back in the long grass. Oh, yes, he would! He docked me several weeks' wages at the Weede Gym. For a while, he seemed to enjoy allocating all the dirty jobs of the day and placing me under curfew for practically the rest of that semester – a wise move with a naïve and wearisome freshman like me. The coach also cleverly threw in additional studies at my favourite place – the library! He knew how to get through to rebellious runners.

I gladly accepted these extra hours of 'Community Service.' Thankfully, I had been let off lightly, and I knew it! I had survived the Partygate and Pizzagate. My companion and I had lived to tell the tale and have been forever grateful. It could have all been much more serious. Deadly serious.

Rumour has it that following 'Partygate 1980,' my colleague ended up a teetotaller after his brush with death and danger and has never looked at another drink. As for me, I've been off Pizza ever since. Even a magical 'meat feast' couldn't tempt me.

I don't even take a starter, and I don't own an automatic.

The Currier family c.1980.

Chapter Fourteen –
Thanksgiving and Christmas with the Curriers

Unquestionably, my favourite remembrance of being in America was, for me, the season called Thanksgiving. A Federal holiday celebrated on the fourth Thursday in November, Thanksgiving was created as a day of appreciation for the harvest blessing and the preceding year. What is incredibly uplifting about this holiday period is that people experiencing poverty, rejection, and loneliness are considered, cared for, and given food and shelter. When I arrived, I knew little about this reflective outreach, which encouraged Americans to think of others less fortunate. Of course, I had experienced celebrating the Harvest period at home, a similar idea, but not quite an American Thanksgiving.

Growing up, I recall some excellent Harvest services when the Presbyterian church I attended in Bangor was decorated with fruit and vegetables and many other foods. My friends and I always arrived before the choir and filled a few bags with apples and oranges. I'm not sure it was allowed, but we were growing lads, and it kept us going during the service. It also stopped me from further local Apple relocation! (There was an apple orchard on Hamilton Road in those days, and I was continually chased out of it by a man who, if he had caught me just once, would probably have beaten the living daylights out of me.)

Harvest is a beautiful season. It reminds me of the words of the well-known hymn, "We plough the fields and scatter the good seed on the land, but it is fed and watered by God's almighty hand." It's always good to give thanks and be grateful for what we have, a concept I would learn much more of in America. Thanksgiving wasn't exclusively celebrated in American churches. It spread well beyond the doors of the sanctuary. It was about community and charity across the board. Even today, various societies have annual food drives, and many charitable distributions are made. The Salvation Army's Christian organisation enlists volunteers to serve Thanksgiving dinners to hundreds of people in different locations in the United States. And, of course, today, food banks abound, sadly.

There is something incredibly spiritual and humbling about Thanksgiving in America when it comes to helping the poor, the less well-off, and the needy. I remember how the atmosphere in the city seemed to change overnight. A feel-good factor emerged, producing extraordinary kindness during this unique holiday season. There was a more friendly, less selfish spirit at work, and you could genuinely sense greater unity and goodwill. Of course, if anyone needed assistance and a hand of friendship, it was yours truly in 1980. Miles from home, I was expecting a barren and lonely vacation in Pittsburg, yet nothing could have been further from the truth. I became a primary recipient of this most generous of seasons, called Thanksgiving. As the November holiday approached, I faced the prospect of life alone in that tiny 'prefab' near the campus. I was dreading it. I was glad of the accommodation, but with two sports-obsessed athletes like Jack and I living there, the place was a bit of a shack. We didn't do 'Domestic' and the place was a bit of a tip most of the time. The outside needed cleaning. The inside, occupied by two untidy sports guys, was even worse. I think I was more cluttered than Jack. When he arrived home one evening and saw one of my training shoes hanging from the bedroom light, it stopped him in his tracks.

Bewildered, he commented: "I take it that's modern art!"

I don't recall bringing a girl back to that shack; she would have run a mile. It was dark inside, bordering on downright depressive. Clothes lay everywhere, and there was a strange, fusty smell, not helped by Cannabis blowing through the windows from across the street. The food cupboards were frequently bare as we often ate out. And who could forget the scent of Jack and my training shoes? The truth is, I hated being on my own there. I had no company other than Jack, who was out of the house most of the time, like me. Once, when what felt like a mini tornado blew through the city, I remember our little house almost split in two. I was under the bed, perhaps not the recommended place to take shelter from a small hurricane. We didn't have a basement, and the bedroom had big windows that faced Darryl's party porch next door.

Watching what he and his companions got up to each night provided me with no shortage of entertainment when I couldn't sleep. Speaking of Darryl, even he and his party pals wouldn't be around that same Thanksgiving while Jack was heading to his folks' house for some of Norma Jean's legendary chicken and chips. Who could blame him? The entire campus was like a ghost town for several days. It was shaping up to be a lonely and demoralising time for me. I considered going home, but funds wouldn't allow it. Anyway, I had only been there a few months. I'm not sure I would have returned if I had gone home at that stage.

And so, thousands of miles away from my family in Ireland, I desperately needed the proverbial TLC, and I needed it badly, and I needed it now. I wasn't looking forward to the break as much as some, but I needn't have worried. Everything changed after I received the sweetest invitation – the opportunity to spend Thanksgiving and Christmas with the Curriers.

They lived in an affluent city area and were a close family, unified and welcoming. I had watched American families enjoy significant feasts and fun around the dinner table on TV back in Ireland, and it always looked inspirational. American houses seemed more extensive than home, and the meals were frequently supersized, which suited Moi down to the ground. So here I was, about to have the opportunity to experience first-hand what Thanksgiving in America was all about.

It happened this way. One November night, while I was sitting in the dark to save electricity and feeling quite hungry, a knock came on the door. "What are you doing for Thanksgiving this year?" asked Scott.

"I hadn't thought about it; why?" I replied, lying through my teeth, of course.

It was all I had been thinking about.

Instead, Scott insisted: "You're coming to our house to spend it with us." "You're kidding!" I gasped. It was a genuine gasp. Not a fake one. I was deeply touched and even surprised, but secretly relieved. For weeks, I'd been reading my airmails repeatedly to curtail homesickness. I used to wait for them to arrive like I was waiting on a large cheque. They were mainly from Mum and my perfect cousin, Katrina, from Holywood, Co Down, although Katrina and I had always acted like an A-list couple from Hollywood (with two Ls). Before America, I enjoyed several nights out with Katrina. Everyone assumed she was my girlfriend. A finalist in Miss Northern Ireland, she was a natural beauty, increasing my inflated ego. But the truth was, I was dating her friend, Sonia, also from Holywood, and another one of those Catholic girls my mother managed to chase from our home.

Having told Mum, I was for an athletics meeting, Sonia would pick me up in her little cream beetle car at the end of the street, and off we'd go, but it was no more than a teenage fling. Following my move to America, Katrina would keep me informed about how she and Sonia were doing and who was going out with whom, which made me envious when I learned of all the fun they were having. Contrast this to my lonely state in America - the intervention of Scott and his family would prove critical in helping me settle in my new abode. Unknown to Scott, even by November, I still suffered from homesickness and prayed for a minor miracle, which arrived. It's incredible how one door knock can change your whole outlook.

"My folks are adamant; you are coming to spend the entire vacation with us," added Scott, who received no further objections from me. Never one to look a gift horse in the mouth, I jumped at the opportunity, and what a time it proved! Awaiting me was the most fantastic food and entertainment. I still recall the large table and quintessential all-American meal of turkey, cranberry sauce, vegetables, potatoes, and pie. It was awesome, as they say in America. It also turned out to be merely a warmup to Christmas Dinner in December, when I would be invited back to Scott's and his family's homes for the entire Christmas period.

A timely intervention of great grace had visited my young life, and I was so grateful, but should I have been surprised? I was in America, a place known as the home of hospitality and the best food. I had arrived in a country where goodness and kindness shone through on more than one occasion. American novelist Thomas Wolfe once remarked, "America is a great country, the only country. It is the only place where miracles not only happen but where they happen all the time."

I could not disagree. I experienced big and small miracles before and after my arrival in the United States. And so, I began to count them individually, and it surprised me how blessed I had been. For example, I had someone older and more worldly-wise to look out for me, like Roddy. In Jack, I also had someone to live with who helped meet many of my needs. It's always good to have a big brother figure at various stages of your life, someone to look after you when you need a wiser and more experienced head. I lost count of the times Roddy and Scott said things like, "Be careful, John, I wouldn't go there," or my favourite line, when I would show interest in a female athlete -"She's not for you, Kid." That was something they got tired of saying. Even though I didn't always take their well-meaning advice, I was thankful for friends who saw danger ahead and warned me about it.

Being able to race in the national championships, having been dogged by injury before the competition, also felt like fortune, while finding a friend like Scott Currier, who made my time in America memorable for many reasons, was only one of the incredible joys I experienced during my time in the USA. Of course, little did the Curriers realise that those dinner invitations, especially at Thanksgiving, not only helped feed me but also made me feel incredibly welcome. Here was reassurance that I was finally settling in Pittsburg. Before then, I didn't feel like I truly belonged there until suddenly, I had an adopted home, a family, and a future.

Inviting me to their home was more than a small act of kindness. It gave me a sense of belonging. It breathed a spirit of generosity and helped me be more considerate of others, which is what Thanksgiving is all about. I had never given that concept enough thought. Before this, I was probably too selfish and dominated by the tunnel vision required to become a top-class athlete to think of others, but that Thanksgiving invitation opened a closed mind and heart. It is always good to hear of kindness, but when someone shows it to us, it can transform our entire way of thinking. It genuinely can produce a supernatural result.

After feeling lonely, I suddenly liked America because of its food, drink, friendship, and family values. I didn't look for those airmails anymore. Pittsburg became my home from home, and it was terrific! Even Coach

Suenram's brutal training sessions were no longer daunting. I found the courage, dug in, and decided to fit in, come what may. It was time to 'Man up,' and I did. During that memorable Thanksgiving holiday, we played games and told jokes, with me the brunt of most of them. I remember enlightening the Curriers about 'the situation' and culture in Ireland, leaving Scott less interested in 'The Troubles' and more amused at my pronunciation of the word Film.

"It's a 'movie', John," he would say with a giggle, "not a Fulum,"

Meanwhile, I enjoyed hearing them all repeat American phrases like: "Oh really", "That's awesome", and "God dang, it", a classic saying in the Midwest I found amusing. I sensed remarkable goodwill at Thanksgiving and, perceived how people were genuinely grateful for all they had received. During those holiday feasts, I was like the stranger in the story of the Good Samaritan who had been rescued and cared for. I recall how Scott's dad was incredibly kind-hearted. He was extremely gentle and caring – the father figure anyone would wish for. I didn't feel worthy, but the Curriers insisted I receive their hand of friendship. I felt like a homeless man privileged to be invited to dine with a King. I didn't deserve such fortune, but I had found it and most gratefully accepted it.

On reflection, my good fortune was like the lame man in the second book of Samuel when King David showed extraordinary kindness to Mephibosheth, the son of a man called Jonathan and the grandson of the great King Saul. The story tells of how Mephibosheth was only five years old when Saul and his sons died in battle at Mount Gilboa. His nurse picked him up and fled, but she dropped the child, injuring both his feet and making him lame for the rest of his life.

Many years later, when the boy was in his twenties, David became King and started to inquire about any descendants of King Saul. Instead of planning to kill the previous King's line, as was the custom in those days, David wanted to honour them both in memory of his friend Jonathan, even out of respect for Saul. Immediately, Saul's servant Ziba told David how Jonathan's son Mephibosheth was living in Lo Debar, meaning "place of nothing." Immediately, David summoned Mephibosheth to court. Imagine how Mephibosheth must have felt. He would likely have assumed he was being called to die. Instead, the King said to him: "Don't be afraid, for I will surely show you kindness for the sake of your father Saul, and you will eat continually at my table."

Eating at the King's table wasn't just to enjoy the country's best food; it also meant falling under the protection of a friend and the ruler of the Kingdom. To him, having his grandfather's land restored was unheard of kindness. History records how Mephibosheth lived in Jerusalem and ate continually at the King's table from that point on. He was safe and secure, and cared for. Mephibosheth was loved!

Of course, Mephibosheth is an Old Testament picture of someone who discovers similar kindness through the sacrifice of another. I have lost count of the times I have received such kindness, and always when needed most. Yet, never was this compassion more appreciated than in the winter of 1980. With snow on the ground, a struggling student away from home for the first time, and feeling lonelier by the day, I found incredible favour in a strange country. I had no table to eat at until the Curriers' invitation changed my world.

How blessed was I to receive such benevolence from this American family who didn't really know me and had never met my folks, yet they treated me as one of their own and reached out at Thanksgiving and Christmas, with the hand of friendship and fellowship. Maya Angelou wrote: "After the word love, kindness is the most beautiful word." I couldn't argue. Their kindness shone through and touched the heart of a stranger like me! – a homesick student in a foreign land. It's over forty years since then, but that act of humanity and goodness is as fresh today as ever.

Since then, I have never underestimated the importance of the kindness shown to me by the Currier family or the importance of reaching out to the vulnerable. Those hidden helpers in my life have demonstrated similar charity and taught me to become a secret helper in the lives of others when I have the opportunity, and sometimes even when I don't. Neither have I questioned anything that fails to work out as planned. Time and the world are ever in flight.

Chapter Fifteen - On the Road Again

The Midwest of America was not only a sports haven for young athletes like me; country music was abundant back then, too. Every bar, restaurant and shop blasted out the top country hits, and young America loved it. Country music has maintained a solid and varied history in America for over a century. It all began with traditional folk in the Southern United States but has spread globally and is today enjoyed by millions. It is fair to say that country music represents a large slice of American culture and has motivated music lovers everywhere to embrace it.

I, too, joined this global club, having once mocked the mere thought of country music. I remember my dad was heavily into 'country sounds' before my departure to America, though I never quite got it. He was into global celebrities like Glen Campbell, Johnny Cash, and Jim Reeves. I marvelled at how he would use a cushion for an accordion while listening to Charlie Pride's famous song 'Crystal Chandeliers.' It's amazing what a few whiskeys and cushions can do to a person late at night! When my mother was in Australia, these country and western gigs took place frequently at our home as my genial dad invited half the street home for a good old singsong. Had Mum known what was happening in our house, she would have been on the next plane home!

I was into soul and disco music then, 'getting down on it' with groups like Kool and the Gang, Tavares, The Drifters, The Spinners, and the Jackson Five. So, I never expected to enjoy country music, but my taste soon changed after a few unforgettable barn dances and fun-packed nights out in the States. 'Lookin' for Love (In All the Wrong Places)' by country star Johnny Lee was a great song. As Johnny once said, "I were wookin' for love", and some of those lyrics summed up my failed attempts at finding romance in America.

RUNNING AWAY

It was during the 1960s that the outlaw country movement began, with notable names and artists such as Johnny Cash, Waylon Jennings and the without equal Willie Nelson. He was undoubtedly the most prominent and prolific music star I recall. Nelson's 9th Country and Western No. 1 hit "On the Road Again" in November 1980, was one of his most famous songs and a memorable tune throughout my time in America. It even won him a Grammy Award for Best Country Song. Funnily enough, like Johnny Lee's hit, some of the lyrics in Nelson's award-winning track described life to a tee at that stage. Following the Christmas break, the track team and I were about to be 'on the road again' and 'going to places I'd never seen and seeing things I may never see again.'

It was bitterly cold by then. Long gone were the sweltering training runs that had me seeing double. Instead, we were offered balaclavas to help with the minus-ten temperatures. It was alarming to see up to 12 masked men set off for their morning run.

"You came to the States to escape The Troubles, John, but they seem to be following you here," Roddy quipped.

Cold or not, we were training regularly and about to visit somewhere I had not only dreamed of but hadn't yet had the opportunity to see. A youthful desire of mine was about to come true in spectacular style – none other than a visit to Texas and, more notably, the city of Dallas. They say everything comes to those who wait, and never more so in my case. I had watched dozens of episodes of the Dallas series before leaving Ireland and continued to watch in America. I'd even had my hopes dashed of visiting the great city when my first scholarship choice fell through.

Yet here I was, finally assured that I would soon be on my way to see the city of my dreams. I was beside myself with excitement. I would ultimately witness first-hand the place and city I had come to love so much on TV, but not as anticipated. For a start, we were only there briefly, giving me precious little time to see everything, while, to my consternation, Dallas didn't turn out to be the place I imagined.

We travelled there by bus, and the changing scenery was stunning. It seemed like every state was different yet equally beautiful. As we crossed into Dallas, the motorway reminded me of the one in Paris: chaotic, crazy, and sheer mayhem. We had arrived for a track meet the following day, but I had only one thing on my mind – racing into the city centre to see if I could spot J.R. and Bobby's office. So, I, for once, ignored the orders not to leave the accommodation we were staying at and wandered down the road. A quick dander never hurt anyone, right?

Wrong Move!

Before long, I was lost and ended up in an area where I would soon discover I wasn't welcome. Never a person to let previous disappointments get in my way, I had sneaked into Dallas alone, half expecting to bump into Bobby, JR and Cliff. I kid you not; I was half-deluded about that series, Dallas! I hadn't given up on Southfork, not by a long chalk! West Texas had come and gone, but I still longed for a tea party with Lucy, Sue Ellen, and Pam. But rather than meet the cast of my favourite soap opera or come anywhere near that beautiful American ranch, I was confronted by a well-built black man who threatened to kill me because I was white and on the wrong side of town. Suddenly, my view of Dallas changed, and the incident opened my eyes regarding the similarities between America and Ireland.

The racial or religious divisions existed well outside of my country. In my case, I was familiar with political intolerance, having grown up surrounded by it at home, where having the most bombed hotel in Europe ('The Europa') was seen as a badge of honour. Remarkably, the guests would be asked if they would like a wake-up call, as if they needed one! I was familiar with the religio-political divide in Ireland and my own northern province, but highly ignorant of the racism I would experience in the United States. Yes, I had heard of the Civil Rights Movement and was very aware of names like Martin Luther King, Rosa Parks, and Frederick Douglass (1818-1895) and his association with Belfast, having visited the city in 1846 and being most impressed by the citizens.

I knew their stories and had heard of their struggles. Yes, and even that of Stagecoach Mary, too!

However, I was still shocked by the ongoing deep-rooted division I experienced between blacks and whites in Dallas and other places in America that I visited. It saddened and grieved me because racism can be just as destructive as religious prejudice. I had never thought of Dallas as anything other than a white city in the state of Texas, where the people wore cowboy hats and big boots, and so expected to see white faces as the norm, but my perception was mistaken! I'd watched a little too much of that soap opera. Instead of finding Ray Krebbs, I ran into a regular Mike Tyson.

My first experience of segregation between races emerged while walking down a long, empty Dallas Street, feeling hungry but not necessarily concerned about being lost, which I was. I had earned a few dollars from my work at the Weede Gym, and they were burning a hole in my pocket. Searching for a restaurant, I spotted a sign and entered the building by the back stairs. It led me to a surprisingly busy cafe, which seemed odd as few people were on the street outside. That street was as long and deserted as a Sunday morning sidewalk. The eeriness ought to have alerted me.

Nonetheless, I selected what I wanted, put it on a tray, and proceeded to the counter. I still hadn't realised I was the only white person in the eatery. The man at the till blanked me several times, and I remember feeling upset that other people who had arrived after me were already served.

What was wrong?

Am I invisible?

I knew I wasn't because everyone was looking at me.

Then, before I could say anything, a black male with a dark cap snarled at me and said, "Friend, you either have a sense of humour or a death wish. Which is it, man?"

"What do you mean" I nervously responded, to which he quickly added, "Take your little white butt out of here as fast as possible, or you're going on a journey you won't return from."

It was an invitation I couldn't refuse. The penny finally dropped, and I didn't require additional persuasion. I suddenly remembered the maxim - when in Rome! Being young and naïve, I was clearly out of my depth and void of common sense, and I think he knew this. This kind and compassionate gentleman must have given me the benefit of the doubt. THE Coach LET ME HAVE IT, and some, when I eventually found my way back to the hotel and relayed my story. Even recent impressive performances couldn't exempt me from hearing how he felt, and he was right. I had placed myself and him in danger by wandering off alone, and without permission.

But that was far from the end of my antics in Dallas. Another incident on my way back left me looking and feeling equally foolish. As I approached the front doors of large department stores and government buildings, I would lift my hands high, expecting to be searched by security. It was second nature to raise my hands. It was the norm in Belfast, and most parts of Northern Ireland insisted upon this ritual during 'The Troubles.' I'd been doing this for several years. People weren't allowed into the premises unless thoroughly searched by the army or other authorised security personnel. But with no security present at the doors of the premises in Dallas and standing with my hands held high for apparently no reason, all I received were strange looks from shoppers entering and leaving those stores. Thank God there was no video of it!

I overheard one lady tell her friend, "God help him; I don't think the young boy is too well," something that may not have been far from the truth, as it happened. Unknown to her and me, I was suffering a hangover from 'The Troubles,' a memory that has persisted throughout my life. I had left for America, but the conflict and the consequences hadn't left me.

Even today, many decades later, I still get flashbacks of uncomfortable and unnerving events during the crises. Is this a common thing? Many people and nations struggle with trauma or Post Traumatic Stress Disorder (PTSD) following horrific events, and the people of my generation in Northern Ireland are no different. Soldiers serving in war-torn countries and civilians caught up in such wars are often left disturbed by such events.

It is telling that while 'The Troubles' have been over for numerous years, many who lived through that period get flashbacks about what occurred as they grew up. Research has shown that it is most likely that the mental health of the population of Northern Ireland was substantially affected by the civil upheaval. Whether this is attributable to the violence or other aspects of the conflict is unclear, but many people carry the scars of 30-plus years of war.

It is called memory. Countless people, including me, have been able to forgive the armed militias for what they did to our beautiful land and people, but forgetting is another matter. Sometimes, it is easier to forgive than forget. Even now, Northern Ireland is a post-conflict society with generational trauma. When you've lived through and experienced life-changing incidents such as Enniskillen, the Omagh Bombing, Bloody Sunday, and Bloody Friday, total recovery is not assured, no matter what road you take or which part of the community you originate from. The trauma often goes with you.

I was reporting for BBC Northern Ireland when the Omagh bomb exploded on 15 August 1998, killing 29 people, plus unborn twins, and injuring 220 others. Like many of my fellow citizens, that sun-splashed afternoon is seared into my memory. I haven't been able to speak about this day and atrocity for over a quarter of a century. The 500lb car bombing, carried out by the Real IRA, ripped through the heart of the town and became the deadliest single incident in the history of The Troubles. If there was any consolation following the tragedy, it was the fact that the bombing caused outrage both locally and internationally and probably helped to speed up the peace process in Northern Ireland.

I recall this day well because I was reporting on an Irish League football (soccer) match between Glentoran and Omagh Town at the Oval, Glentoran's home stadium in East Belfast. When the players returned for the second half, I sensed something was wrong with both sets of players, especially the Omagh team. The players had no interest in even passing the ball to each other. Word had spread about the events of that day, and following the final whistle, which recorded a 2-0 win for Glentoran, I spent the rest of the evening filing report after report, not about a football match but about the state of the players, coaches, and everyone at the game. That day, there was a darkness and sadness that none of us had ever felt and will never hopefully feel again. Before the bombing, hope sprang eternal that things were changing, only for the scourge of violence to strike again and lunge the province back into despair.

These atrocities, of course, along with many others, are a reminder not only of how far Northern Ireland has come but hopefully will never return to. And also, of course, just how fragile is the nature of our hard-won peace.

John McCreedy

In Dallas, I was saddened to learn that just as there was an intense political divide in my own country, resulting in terrible atrocities like Omagh, and Bloody Sunday, America retained its legacy of division between blacks and whites, and seemingly, some had not progressed from the time of the Civil Rights movement.

However, things were a lot more progressive at Pittsburg State University, where the narrative of racism was challenged during my time in America. PSU appeared to be a place that embraced all colours, races, and religions. Our group of athletes consisted of people from different states and countries with varying skin colours. If ending racism was Garfield Weede's influence, it was undoubtedly positive and working. It also exposed me to something I had never adequately experienced before - multiculturalism. We hear much about that word today, yet in 1980, I was gently shown how to accept people of all descriptions.

These game-changing individuals' names, faces, and huge personalities are forever imprinted in my heart. They helped shape my thinking. No one can meet people like that in life and forget them. Characters like Rico, White Owl, Herm, Currier, Gaynor, and Suenram, to name but a few. To a man, they knew how to make someone feel at home and, part of their "club," town, and city.

I still recall being introduced to 'Hollywood's, a well-known and legendary watering hole in the city. Here, I learned about college football, unity in college life, and, dare I say it, even the facts of life! These guys were up for anything!

It didn't matter what environment you hailed from or your skin colour; if you made it down to Hollywood's and their table, you were welcomed with open arms as part of the family.

Nevertheless, due to the increase in technology and other areas, today, the world is global, but back then, many nations still lived in relative backwaters, even parts of America. If there was one thing I discovered during my time at Pitt State, it was how little I knew about American culture and how little Americans then appeared to know about the situation back home in Ireland. We were educating each other.

Despite almost everyone having a distant cousin from Cork to Dublin and even Belfast, most people I encountered knew very little about the civil strife known as 'The Troubles.' Every day, it was international news, but there was clearly a lack of deeper understanding about what was really going on between those fighting for Irish reunification and those who wished to remain British. Eventually, I realised that politics and culture were a two-way street.

Since those days, we've seen significant changes in Ireland with the Anglo-Irish Agreement and the Good Friday Agreement, yet sadly, community tensions still exist. Back in 1980, after I arrived in America, I began to question the polarisation and deep suspicions in Ireland. It was remarkably liberating. My bubble had been burst, and my eyes were opening. I had come to America to run on a track, yet suddenly, I was learning to run well in life and get along with people, regardless of background. Of course, while Ireland had problems, especially in the North, it has always been known for its hospitable, friendly, and welcoming people.

Notwithstanding attempts to eradicate bigotry in Ireland and racial prejudice in America, the division between white people and the African American community sadly persists, while my homeland isn't out of the woods either, despite the Peace Process that generally and thankfully continues to hold.

My trip to Dallas and subsequent experiences taught me that nearly every city and nation has its religious and racial divisions – problems caused by often, very long-standing historical disputes and events. Everywhere has a past and faces a future of challenges. Ending such separations, even dealing with the fallout, has proved easier said than done for most. We are all still a work in progress, but the road to reconciliation must and will continue. Peace is always preferable to strife. Meanwhile, I would be on the road again within no time—next stop, Oklahoma, and the arrival of a most unwelcome guest.

Chapter Sixteen - A Snake in the Night

The indoor track season was in earnest, and we were bound for the great city of Oklahoma long before it experienced that awful atrocity - the Oklahoma Bombing. This incident was the deadliest act of terrorism in US history until the September 11 attacks on the Twin Towers in New York in 2001. The bombing, however, was a purely domestic affair – a truck bombing of the Alfred P. Murrah Federal Building in Oklahoma City on April 19, 1995, coincidentally the second anniversary of the infamous and fiery end to the Waco Siege in Texas. However, the city is also famous for its positive accomplishments, such as the musical Oklahoma, written by the duo of Rodgers and Hammerstein, and, of course, the birthplace of the shopping trolley! Back in the Eighties, I recall it as a friendly city. However, I am still left cowering due to what happened on the weekend I visited, so I don't remember it for its tourist attractions, scenery, or athletic eminence but for something slightly more sinister – and personal.

Coach Suenram, always a man who counted the dollars and cents to ensure our track team stayed within budget, had put some of us up in houses belonging to my fellow athletes. It seemed like a good idea and would prevent a bill from a local hotel. I was selected to room with one of our teammates, Robert, a tall, leggy guy with long blonde hair who always gave his best. It was like running beside Bjorn Borg, except Robert didn't wear a headband. His stride was worth two of mine, but I still always finished ahead of him. Running had nothing to do with the length of your legs! However, staying at Robert's house presented an excellent opportunity to experience further American hospitality and visit a new part of the United States. I had seen Oklahoma in the country and Western movies on TV, but here was a chance to ride into town and check the place myself. What wasn't to like about that? I was excited.

RUNNING AWAY

The coach had entered me in a 1500-metre indoor event the following day, a race he believed I could impress. Thanks to speed merchants Gaynor and Johnson, I'd been trailed to a higher level, and my speed work had improved significantly. I recall being enthusiastic about this race as it indicated what I could do on faster outdoor surfaces later that year. I wanted to break the four-minute mile before the age of twenty, and here was a chance to see how far away from that illustrious target I was. Nowadays, that wouldn't be too exceptional. After all, 17-year-olds from Australia and Northern Ireland have already run astonishing times of under 3.57. Still, I suspect many athletes would be delighted to break the four-minute mile regardless of age. The great Roger Bannister attained it at 25 when he recorded 3:59.4 in 1954 at Iffley Road in Oxford. Remarkably, that mark has since been lowered by almost 17 seconds, and the world record currently stands at 3:43.13, set by Hicham El Guerrouj of Morocco at age 24 way back in 1999.

Meanwhile, tucked up in our beds early in preparation for the big mile event, I had no idea of the calamity ahead. As darkness fell, Robert and I were given a room to sleep in with twin beds. I have always taken time to fall asleep. I lie and think about things too deeply, keeping me awake longer than I like. And this night was no exception.

On the other hand, Robert swiftly drifted into a deep sleep as I considered the next day's race and many other things. I envied how quickly he could nod off, leaving me to fend for myself in more ways than one. There I was, counting sheep while he snored peacefully. Conscious of every noise around me, suddenly, I became aware of a familiar sound, but not one I expected to catch in a bedroom. It was a strange hissing noise. The lights were out. It was pitch dark. The noise was peculiar. It sounded like…well, I don't even want to go there! I assumed it would stop, so I stayed silent and waited a while. When the disturbance didn't cease but grew louder and more concerning, I knew it was time to act.

"Robert, are you still awake?" I asked.

"Huh," replied Robert.

He wasn't.

There's nothing worse than awakening someone out of their sleep, but this was an emergency, and I had no alternative. I had to do the unthinkable. After stretching out my leg and kicking him, I asked, "Robert, are you still up? What's that strange noise?"

"What noise?" Robert responded.

Robert was used to this sound, so he was probably oblivious.

By now, my heart was racing. Though I thought it improbable, I had a terrible feeling that I knew the sound. It couldn't be, but what if it was? It would be one of my life's scariest moments if I were proven correct. Anyway, I was in Oklahoma, wasn't I? And, in a plush house in the heart of the city centre, not in some jungle somewhere. I was as safe as houses, wasn't I? Nonetheless, I asked again - this time with no shortage of terror in my voice - "Robert, wake up; what is that strange noise in the room?" Finally, he stirred and replied without apology or fear: "Pay no attention; that's just Julie."

"And who is Julie?" I insisted.

Robert rolled over. I knew he heard me, but he didn't want to answer.

"Who the heck is Julie, Robert?" I persisted.
Finally, he broke his silence.

"She's ma' pet snake," came his casual response.

Suddenly, life was out of my control. There was nothing I could do but pray. Have you ever had a time when your body froze in absolute terror? I was stiff with fear. I had always dreaded being anywhere near, let alone sleeping with such a thing, in a blacked-out room. It was a case of: 'I'm an athlete; get me out of here!'

I immediately responded: "Julie, I can live with, but not a snake. Please, Robert, where is the snake? I beg you, put the lights on and take that thing out of here ASAP."

Robert remained utterly detached and uninterested in my dread, describing Julie as "harmless" and, can you believe it, "friendly," no less!

"She wouldn't hurt a fly, John; she's just a baby snake," added the deluded Robert.

"I don't care what you say or think, Robert; in my opinion, there's no such thing as a friendly snake, baby or not. Just get up and get that thing out of here now."

I can't recall if the snake was in a cage or creeping about loose, but who cared! It was in the room. What was happening to me? I cried as I begged my colleague to clear that room in a heartbeat. To my immense relief, Robert finally sensed my anxiety and distress, rose to the occasion, found the snake in the darkness, and put it outside the door. He looked like Crocodile Dundee as he swept it up and took it outside with his bare hands. He had Dundee's callousness, too. He was genuinely amused by my fear of 'so-called' Julie, but I didn't see the funny side of it, not even for a moment.

As I've said, growing up, I was not too fond of snakes. Of course, legend has it that the great patron saint, and National Apostle of Ireland, St Patrick, drove the snakes out of Ireland, a feat worthy of honour and the cherishing of his memory alone. Who would have thought, however, that I would encounter them in a smart house in Oklahoma? Debates have occurred in Ireland for years about Saint Patrick's exact birthplace in Roman Britain and how he single-handedly influenced Ireland for good as a Christian. That night, I wish he'd banished the snakes from Oklahoma as well!

The rest of that night was a nightmare. I couldn't be confident that this 'creature' Robert had cruelly introduced me to would not return, sliding under the door when I was finally asleep. Like in 'Jaws,' I believed it would return worse the second time. "Julie the Revenge" had a ring about it. So, I got up and put my bag and something else with weight across the door, again much to Robert's amusement and apparent lack of concern for my anxiety. He was in stitches now, which incensed me even more. I don't know if he was joking or not, but the following comment was the most concerning:

"Have you any idea how strong a snake is, John? Do you think that little barricade you've built will deter it? Put your head down and fall asleep, and morning will be here before you know it."

"Yeah, right, as if I could do that. Thanks, Robert, for your comfort and encouragement," I moaned.

If only we had stayed in a Hilton or a Marriott. Oh, the bliss of a warm room, double bed and a comfortable night's sleep! Who would have believed my life would be in such mortal danger in a leafy suburb home in Oklahoma? Robert quickly crashed out, and while he snored, I kept guard at that door until dawn. I responded to any noise or sound close by instantly. I heard every animal in the garden that night, but it was the snake I was on high alert for. I didn't close my eyes the entire night, and nothing would persuade me to do so.

Of course, I was exhausted and wanted to nod off several times, but the 'snakes' were too high (forgive the pun), and, remember, according to Robert, it hadn't gone away.

The morning light didn't bring me any real relief, either. Despite an excellent breakfast in the house, I continually looked over my shoulder and disbelieved any notion that "harmless" and "friendly" Julie was securely out the back. I only relaxed when the bus to pick us up for the race pulled out of the driveway, and I knew my snake dilemma was over.

However, even then, I checked underneath the seats in case Julie followed us. She hadn't. The snake was gone, but the utter tiredness from the night before remained in my legs. The exhaustion proved more destructive to my athletic ambitions that day than I could ever have imagined. Even during the warm-up, I could feel my legs like jelly. Not having slept a wink, I was yawning and felt drained, but I had managed to keep my distance from the coach to prevent him from noticing any bags under my eyes. He would naturally assume we had been 'out on the town' and would never fall for a story about a snake keeping me up all night – even though it was 'the God's truth!' Then, the actual moment of truth arrived. My race was called, and I knew it was reality time.

I was not my usual focused self for obvious reasons, and after only a couple of laps, I was already feeling the heat and sliding down the field. I often tried to lead from the front or stay beside the leaders in middle-distance events because I never liked being too far back in case I couldn't close the gap. Only athletes with a great kick can permit gaps to grow and still have enough in the tank to close them when they choose.

This unusual tactic of hanging back made Coach Suneram suspicious. He quickly realised something was wrong. I could hear him shouting from the sidelines for me to "get my act together", but it made no difference. The harder he yelled, the further I fell behind.

Of course, I knew early on that this was one race I would not only lose but would be fortunate to finish. As the race progressed, I fell so far behind the other competitors that I ended up at the back of the field. Right then, I knew how it felt to be last. I had never had that experience. For the first time in my career, I could identify with runners who endure this sort of experience every week but keep participating for whatever enjoyment and challenges it brings them. To them, running was more important than time and winning; they didn't come to break records but to race. They found pleasure in running and the journey, not the destination. I didn't have a similar attitude. I never ran for fun. I ran for results and resultant glory. As McKnight once stated, I saw myself as a runner, not a jogger.

On that uncomfortable day in Oklahoma, however, I felt like the slowest jogger alive, a feeling I never wanted to repeat. Some of the guys who lapped me I had beaten over the country earlier in the season, but this was different. It was a track race, and I hadn't experienced a single wink of sleep for about 36 hours. They may have been talented runners, so it was no shame to be behind some of them, but in my mind, it was still a slippery snake called Julie that put paid to any chances I had of success in Oklahoma. As I crossed the finish line, more through pride, than ability, some 11 seconds slower than my personal best, which over a mile is a considerable distance, I fell to the floor like a wet rag echoing that iconic shot of Roger Bannister the day he broke the four-minute mile.

Of course, the difference was Bannister had something to celebrate while I had something to explain. As the runners cleared the track, I shirked away from the coach, knowing he would come looking for me, and he didn't hold back. I will never forget his face that day. He looked like the Incredible Hulk as he turned from white to green. I hadn't done anything; it was all Robert's fault!!! He was the idiot who made us sleep with a snake. That would be my opening line anyway when I finally came face to face with the outraged Suenram, which wouldn't be too far away.

Catching up with me upstairs, he hollered: "What the heck was that all about, son?"

They say attack is the best defence, so I hit back instantly. "I know you'll find this hard to believe, coach, but you'll never guess what happened last night..."

Coach stared at me and then walked away. I didn't even have the chance to explain, but perhaps just as well. Not only would I have landed poor Robert in hot water, but let's be honest, who believes such a ridiculous tale? "A snake kept me up all night. It was in our bedroom." – who says that?

So, I decided to take it on the chin, say nothing and move on. Coach never found out about the snake shenanigans from the night before, believing instead that I had what we called in athletics "a stinker" that day, which I had, of course.

It still ranks as my worst performance in a pair of spikes. I felt so sorry for Coach Suenram, who had expected much more of me and genuinely wanted me to shine that day. I wanted to shine, too, but I had nothing in the tank. I remember being quite disillusioned on our team bus when we left Oklahoma. I was humbled, upset, and disappointed by the experience, yet relieved to see the back of that snake and now fully aware of how important sleep is to our general well-being. At that time, I vowed never to return to the city of Oklahoma, EVER! I had no desire to go back. It was a case of 'good riddance' to Julie and all things snakes. But as chance would have it, I went back, after all, over thirty years later in 2013, and what an educational experience it turned out to be.

Following the publication of my second book, I was offered the option to promote the manuscript at Barnes and Noble in America and stay in Dallas with my good friend, JW Oliver. He kindly took my wife and myself to the JFK Dallas Memorial and then suggested a trip to the Oklahoma Museum, now a tribute to those who lost their lives during the terror attack in 1995. At first, I was hesitant about re-encountering 'Julie,' but I was intrigued to see the city again. Both museums were eye-opening experiences, especially Oklahoma, a fascinating tour and a beautifully sensitive remembrance venue. In all my years visiting such places, I don't recall anywhere having such a moving effect on me.

The memorial garden for those who lost their lives was tastefully created, but it also told its own story. If walls could talk, these walls did. They challenged everyone about how precious human life is and how, as a God-given gift, no one has a right to take that life away from another. It appealed to people to love and cherish one another while on this earth, no matter how short a time it may prove. As the stories were told of those killed, the lessons learned were striking and confronting.

I remember well the words written on a wall at the Oklahoma Museum: "We come here to remember those who were killed, those who survived and those who changed forever. May all who leave here know the impact of violence. May this memorial offer comfort, strength, peace, hope and serenity."

Those words resonated so much with me and my wife. Like Oklahoma, Belfast has moved on most fearlessly from 'The Troubles.' We had some understanding of this situation, having lived through our difficulties in Northern Ireland. We knew what it was like to lose friends and loved ones and how difficult it can be to recover individually and collectively as an island.

So, even though my first visit to Oklahoma was somewhat eventful, to put it mildly, and unsuccessful regarding my athletic ambitions, my second trip there was enlightening and informative. A return visit to this fascinating city revealed much about the place and myself. The people had strength, resolve, and a deep character. I was truly inspired and left the city with a much better impression and hope.

They say never go back. In my experience, it has proven not always to be true.

Chapter Seventeen - The Last Lap

That slippery snake wasn't the only reason I struggled in Oklahoma. The tiredness and lack of fight I displayed were symptomatic of another, more ominous foe—a chronic and career-ending injury. Shortly after we arrived in Arkansas for another track event, it became clear that all was not well with me. I was still experiencing severe calf trouble and could hardly put my feet on the ground when running and performing. I had never fully admitted to the coach or my training partners how badly my legs were playing up.

Athletes are proud people, and I was prouder than most. I didn't want anyone to know I had issues. I felt it would be an admission of failure and could end my scholarship. Had the time come to Fess Up? Not me! I carried it with me and said nothing. But my worst fears still came to pass. That race in Arkansas was not only the last lap in America - unthinkably, it would prove the final lap of my athletic career. As I struggled to complete the race, I knew I was in trouble and sensed an endpoint long before it happened.

RUNNING AWAY

Of course, the thought of never fully taking part in a competitive track race ever again would have been inconceivable at that point.

Unaware of the disappointment ahead, I had intended to beat the injury and go on to fulfill my dreams. However, the exasperation with injury was getting to me, but I had always assumed it was temporary. So, out of frustration, I lost it and partied all night in Arkansas. I threw caution to the wind and said, "No Way!"

My feeble frame had taken enough, and I reacted badly. The excruciating pain became a distraction. Following our athletics meeting, which went well for PSU, some track teams were invited to a house party, although most had the good sense to say no. We had to return to Pittsburg for training the following morning; nevertheless, I and a colleague who remains nameless, dared to defy Coach Suenram and attend this 'well-publicised' overnight blast in Arkansas.

The following day, my partner in crime was nowhere to be found, leaving me stranded alone in a city I didn't know. Remember, I had once become lost in Dallas and, by the skin of my teeth, had made it out of there alive, but now I was lost in Arkansas. In the end, and by great good fortune, my rebellious teammate and I ran into each other and returned to Pittsburg, although not in the best shape. That morning, we stumbled embarrassingly across the campus entrance towards the Weede Gymnasium in front of the entire track team and Coach Suenram. They were lined up like the army cadet squad in "By Dawn's Early Light" – a famous episode of Columbo. We were not only late. The track had ended for the day. Suenram's eyes were focused on us both. He looked like he would explode, but instead kept calm and, with composure, announced: "My office, guys."

If the coach called us aside, it was one thing: if he called us to his office, we knew we would either be congratulated or grilled. On this occasion, it wasn't the former. The guys whispered sarcastically and smirked as they knew what was coming. Only Roddy seemed to care. With a worried look, he crossed himself and appeared to pray on our behalf. Right to the end, Roddy was such a good guy! Once in full flow, the coach seemed much harder on my colleague than me due to his older status. "How could you have led a first-year student from Ireland like him astray?" insisted Coach Suenram - as if anyone could have stopped that!

"I would have expected more of you," growled Coach.

College antics and guilt aside, I enjoyed my night out, and the dressing down by Coach was probably worth it. I was burnt out by too much road-running from the tender age of thirteen. Churning out between 70 and 100 miles per week, every step had taken its toll on me and my light frame. I had made countless sacrifices for the sport and was mentally tired as well as physically shattered. I needed to let off some steam.

Despite any early ability I'd shown, my frail frame was falling apart. I didn't fully understand it until later when I read the life story of the middle-distance world record holder Sebastian Coe. His father, Peter Coe, an engineer by profession, refused to allow his son to run above thirty or forty miles per week until he was sixteen. Even until his late teens, Coe focused more on speedwork than stamina. It was an approach that served him well as he became a middle-distance legend. I often regretted not following a similar pattern, although I am unsure if that would have prevented the excruciating pain in my legs. It was essentially an injury sent to end any early promise I'd shown.

The truth was, when I should have been approaching my peak, I was done.

Finished.

My athletics career was over, even in those last few weeks in America. No matter how frequently my mind remained positive, my body said 'No more.'

My coaches on each side of the Atlantic – Tony McKnight and Dave Suenram - were exceptional, and I was so blessed to meet both men. They impacted my life in so many more ways than sports. I would have done anything to please them both, but destiny sometimes intervenes in ways we cannot prevent, and a curveball was about to cause havoc in my young life. The hindrance from injury caused me to lose interest in training, and in the last few weeks of my American venture, I embraced a new sport - sunbathing on the front lawn to try and allow my legs to heal. The grass was so long it grew onto the street, but I don't recall being ashamed or shy as my dog-tired white body lay prostrate in front of the passing talent and the entire neighbourhood. I was the colour of a milk bottle, but I didn't seem to mind. We didn't get much sun in Ireland, and I wanted to return looking tanned and healthy.

I had borrowed Roddy's music cassette player to help me through those last few painful and lonely days in the States, and, according to him, he never got it back. Though we both knew it was long gone, Roddy still asked for it in his sixties.

Imagine!

I've told him to "get over it" and "move on", but he finds it hard. Even before he left to follow the athletes on the Irish team at the World Championships in Budapest in 2023, Roddy again reminded me of that beloved music centre. He must have worshipped that darned thing! I'm convinced his mother bought it for his eighteenth birthday, or it cost him a fortune! Or, maybe a childhood sweetheart had given it to him as a going-away present. Whatever, it came in handy to me.

I missed the last few crucial races of the season in America, not through neglect but due mainly to sheer agony and demoralisation. I had a plan, however. I was determined, at that stage, to get help when I went home to Ireland for the summer and then return to America stronger, fitter, and more single-minded than ever at the end of August. Unfortunately, that plan never materialised. To my surprise, providence took over from that point on. Another agenda and pathway for me to follow showed up, and I had no alternative but to run towards it. Everyone has their life lane to run in, and I would find mine, but only with a fight to leave athletics.

Unsurprisingly, one man who refused to give up on me was Tony McKnight. After returning to Belfast, he advised me to take time off and rest. He also helped set up a series of meetings for me with a top sports doctor at the prestigious Royal Victoria Hospital in Belfast. These sessions continued for months, but with little training, no races, no improvement, and no real, clear diagnosis of what was causing my leg problems, the future looked bleak. In those days, athletics was an amateur sport. We didn't run for the money, and funding was virtually non-existent.

It was a different world then. The resources, knowledge channels, and understanding of the needs of young athletes were in their infancy. The whole world of sports injury and recovery as a Specialism in its own right was also at an embryonic stage. If I may be forgiven for the pun, science has come on 'leaps and bounds' since.

Friends and other people around me were adamant that I should finish my education and get a job. I couldn't afford private operations. Even if that was the definitive answer to my injury problems, my argument was: how could I part with a sport that had been my obsession and focus throughout my teenage years? It was an absurd prospect. And what about that dream of going to the Olympics?

So, despite the pain, I did what any young sportsperson with ambition would do – I battled on, hoping against hope and believing things would change. I tried running again, every day. I ran through the familiar territory of Ward and Castle Parks on my return and the track, looking for improvement, but the discomfort continued daily. Some local people in my hometown of Bangor, where I had returned, would see me limping home, discouraged and disappointed, and I knew the end was approaching.

Where, for example, was the young man gliding through Castle and Ward Park like a butterfly without a single hindrance? Where was the carefree school kid with big dreams and the world at his feet? Those days seemed a million miles away.

I needed a "last chance saloon" opportunity to rescue my failing career, and just like that, the great door of opportunity (that had opened to America, out of the blue) arrived again. I received a year-long invitation from an athletic club in Adelaide, Australia. As fortune had it, I could stay rent-free with my Uncle Glyn and Aunt Maureen. They had moved there in the 1970's to escape 'The Troubles' and had a successful life and family in South Australia. My uncle had decided to move there after a paramilitary group blew up the office where he worked in Donegall Street, in Belfast. Fortunately for him and our family, he had been out on his lunch hour, and his life was saved, but some of his colleagues weren't so lucky. Moving overseas is a decision he has never regretted.

I still remember the shock after travelling for well over 24 hours and reaching a country I thought would prove remote, precisely what I required to get my running career back on track. Almost immediately, it didn't turn out like that. On my first morning on a bus travelling into Adelaide, a lady spotted me and, amazingly, asked, "Are you Winnie's son from Bangor?" A reminder – if ever I needed one – that no matter how far I travelled in this world, there would always be someone from Bangor waiting for me who happened to know my mother. If you go to the moon, you will almost certainly meet someone from Bangor who knows Winnie. Mum had eyes everywhere.

Despite the distance, I knew moving to Australia for a year in 1982 would be the final opportunity to save my athletics career, so this trip was vital. If this opportunity failed, it was game over, and the career gone. I was told beforehand by a local coach in Adelaide, who was a part of the Australian national athletics squad, that my legs would respond well if I trained on the soft grass there. The heat and sunshine would help, too. He begged me to come and give it a go. I wasn't so sure, but I was desperate. I thought long and hard about it before giving in. He also promised me total recovery from a 'renowned sports physiotherapist in Adelaide'.

And, so, I saved the money and travelled Down Under, praying for a miracle. Instead, the grass made no difference; I was scammed out of a thousand hard-earned Australian dollars by a bogus encyclopaedia firm that saw me coming, and the physio guy nearly killed me.

I still recall how the Australian police (and my uncle) arrived in Melbourne to console me about my foolishness in working for a scam company. Once the Boys in Blue broke the bad news, my uncle put his arm around my shoulder and commented: "Welcome to the real world, John." To a naive 20-something-year-old, those words were valid, but my uncle's accent was unrecognisable. He'd developed a transatlantic tone – a mix somewhere between golfers Rory McIlroy and Graham McDowell. I hardly recognised him. Speaking of accents, I was just the same after I returned from America. I'd become quite Americanised in my own speech, using terms like "Oh really", "Way to Go," "I have a question," "Is there a trash can here?" - and "Have a nice day!"

New Aussie accent aside, at least my uncle was compassionate, unlike the pseudo little physio appointed to help with my healing process. When I complained about the pain, he would scream at me during vicious sessions: "Shut up, you cowardly little pom, and let me do my job." A derisory term for an immigrant in Australia, a 'pom' is usually a Brit, and

John McCreedy

mainly from England. Lying face down on his wreaking couch, I was writhing in pain, but the physio couldn't have cared less. He kept driving his thumbs into my legs and going on about how much he hated poms and English people. Lovely! As they say in Belfast. Lovely, just lovely!

To say he was brutal is no exaggeration. Maybe following the Ashes cricket series, he had waited to vent his frustration on someone from England, but I was from Northern Ireland. I kept telling him he was picking on the wrong guy and country! Australia had won that year, so why was he so mean to me?

Speaking of Northern Ireland, it was 1982, and the soccer World Cup was underway. I couldn't have been in Australia more inconveniently because, having qualified, my homeland was setting the world alight, beating some top sides, including the mighty Spain. Northern Ireland was rocking! Growing up, my dad took me to Clandeboye Park regularly to watch Irish League club, Bangor, affording me the chance to see one of Northern Ireland's most famous sons, Gerry Armstrong, before his big move to England and eventually Tottenham Hotspur, and the winning goal against Spain for Northern Ireland, in that same year of 1982.

Norman Whiteside, affectionately known as "The Youngest", was only seventeen when he played for Northern Ireland against Yugoslavia in the 1982 World Cup Finals in Spain, usurping Brazilian legend Pele for the "youngest" status. What Northern Ireland fan could ever forget the words of the legendary John Motson in the Estadio Luis Casanova in Valencia as Gerry Armstrong put Northern Ireland ahead - "Arconada...Armstrong". Billy Bingham's boys beat Spain 1-0, creating shockwaves around the planet and sparking celebrations across the country rarely seen before. Two words, two surnames -too good to be true! Yet it all was!

And where was I? In Australia.

I was getting treatment for a sports injury that would prove untreatable. People danced in the streets at home, and I was told about the fantastic celebrations I had missed. Like the rest of Northern Ireland, my brother and sister were on cloud nine while I was on the other side of the world and no further on. I also had to deal with the embarrassment of the scam, which gave me a harsh life lesson. Flying home from Australia, I began to accept that my sports fairytale and athletics adventure were finished.

RUNNING AWAY

I wasn't going to recover from that sports injury, which, throughout my time as an athlete, had threatened to end my career many times and now had precisely done just that. Everyone had high hopes for me, especially my family, so how could I tell them it was over? I also wondered how I would cope without the daily training and goals I had set for myself. It would be such a difficult transition to reality. In many ways, I was emotionally drained. The loss of my athletic career would ultimately feel like a death in the family. I was grieving and would continue to suffer for months and years afterwards. I dreaded tomorrow when the sun would reveal the extent of my shattered dreams on the ground. I had come back to earth with a bump!

However, I knew in my heart of hearts that it was time to face the music and "the real world", as my uncle had indicated. Still, on the plus side, I had experienced one heck of a roller coaster in such a short space of time, which was of some consolation. After all, I couldn't have imagined telling a fourteen-year-old 'me' what journey he was about to embark on. Athletics has taught me that sport is much more than medals and personal bests (PBs).

The places and people it led me to have remained in my memory, as has the travel it provided. So, I knew retirement was the correct decision to protect my physical and mental health. Even the doctors had told me I had little chance of running at a high level again. In short, my calves would never be muscular enough to cope with the impact of high-level running, but, significantly, it would prove far from the end of my dreams. And so, by the end of 1982, I was back in my home in Bangor, where everything began - back to my beloved Ward Park and back to my seat of dreams at Ballyholme. I soon made the transition to a new path, and rather than die, those dreams have only increased over the years. They became different dreams but equally passionate. I saw the ships still sail up Belfast Lough and more planes flying out of Aldergrove, but I wasn't the same person, and for the first time, I had no desire to be on any of them.

I was home, and they say home is where the heart is. The town of Bangor and my country were hard to beat, given all their trials and tribulations. I would discover, like our ancient forefathers, the Celts, that the grass is not always greener!

John McCreedy

I enjoyed my experiences in America and Australia and learned much from them, but there's something about being on home soil. The thing we crave the most is frequently in front of us all along. I always believed Ballyholme to be one of the world's most beautiful and tranquil places, and even more so today.

Of course, there were letters from friends in America, including Scott and Roddy, two guys I loved and admired, but an incredible season in my life had ended. It would never be forgotten, but I had to move on.

As I sat one day contemplating everything that had happened, I noticed a childhood sweetheart I had dated before I left Bangor for America, walking hand in hand with someone else. They seemed so in love. My mother said she would wait outside my house for months after I left for the States, hoping I would suddenly reappear. Even when my mother told her I wouldn't return, she continued coming to the house at night and sitting on our windowsill. Mum felt sorry for her. Yet by the time I did return, my teen lover had found a new love and moved on. Such is life. The train of opportunity will only ever sit for so long in any station. I had taken my chance to leave. I don't regret that, but I lost another opportunity to stay and be happy in love.

"Choices! They make you or break you," Mum had told us.

Providence called, and I chose to obey and go. During that intense time, my lover and friend became the sport of athletics, producing glorious, lasting memories of more than running. Taking the plunge into America was a risk worth taking. It gave me the confidence to achieve in many other areas later in life and opened my eyes to an enhanced way of living. I will always remember the privilege of visiting the United States. America and its people have always been on my mind. The friends and family I made at Pittsburg (with a G) remain as close to my heart today as ever. And, for those few short years that I competed, the sport of athletics gave me hope and purpose during some of the darkest days of my country's history. It may have taken two attempts and a calamitous carry-on to get to the States, but Pittsburg, Kansas, proved the perfect place for me, and I'm so glad I found it. I may not have made it to the Olympics, but I ran a great race, trying. I've lived the American dream and wouldn't change any of it for the world.

Finis.

L-R: Together again in America, 2024 - Roddy, myself and Scott.

Epilogue

I've lost count of how many times people have asked: If I hadn't been so tired and injured, what would America have held for me? Would I still be living there today? Do I feel upset about the injury? Do I feel robbed of something more significant in my life? Do I lie at night and dream, 'what if I had become an Olympic champion?'

The answer is always and emphatically - No.

How could I feel shortchanged and ungrateful for anything? I had the time of my life in the USA and met wonderful people, many of whom remain friends today. Although I may not have appreciated it then, I was undoubtedly one of the luckiest teenagers in Northern Ireland at the start of the Nineteen Eighties.

I may not have realised it, but returning to Ireland following my scholarship opportunity was just the beginning. After the collapse of my athletics career, I was at a major crossroads. So, I decided to finish the recreational management course (which I had begun in America) at a Belfast college, intending to coach rather than run. Having qualified with merit, I did coach briefly.

However, around this time, another idea kept calling and was beginning to take hold of my thoughts. I always had a flair and a passion for writing, and now I had started to envisage – and embrace - the idea of a new path. And one which, with hard work, dedication, and commitment, I might seize and succeed in. One that would combine my penmanship with my devotion to the world of sport. I could run and write. 'Alea Iacta Est'. The die was cast. I had crossed the Rubicon.

And so happily, my new world became the printed page, sports journalism, broadcasting, and later, authorship and Christian ministry.

Joyfully, I've discovered that there's more than one way to realise your ambitions. What athletics wouldn't allow me to experience at the Olympics, my writing has more than compensated for on the page. Even in the face of significant hindrances and unexpected detours, dreams can still come true in the most extraordinary way, yet not always in the way we imagine. Life has taught me that destiny is the faithful friend who always helps us find our way home.

NOTES TO THE TEXT

Chapter One
[1] 'The Troubles' in Northern Ireland are generally considered to have lasted from 1968 to 1998 and are sometimes even colloquially referred to as 'The Thirty Years War' (a reference to the bitter and bloody European conflict between 1618 and 1648, which concluded with The Peace of Westphalia and effectively ended the wars of religion in Europe).
The term itself had been usurped from its original usage, which covered the decade of conflict in Ireland from 1912/1913 -1923 and included both the War of Independence (1919-1921) and the Civil War (1922-1923).
VAR stands for Video Assistant Referee. It's a system where a referee uses video footage to review and potentially overturn decisions made by the on-field referee.

Chapter Two
[2] ('Boy's Brigade: A local and national church-based youth organisation that provided programmes and opportunities for relaxation, sport and development for young people.)

Chapter Three
[3] 'Tartan track...a trademarked, all-weather surfacing made of polyurethane used for track and field competitions.
NI Patois
Beating it back – Fled or Fleeing
Skedaddled – Made off

Chapter Seven
[4] 'An ISDN (Integrated Services Digital Network) is a set of communication standards that allows for the digital transmission of voice and data over a single line connected to the public switched telephone network.

Chapter Eleven
[5] 'Fartlek Training translates to "speed play" in Swedish. It is like interval training. It involves varying pace or difficulty during maintained cardio.

Chapter Fourteen
[6] 'Prefab' was a form of emergency housing constructed for easy fabrication to address the severe housing shortage after the Second World War. They were a common sight in Post-War Belfast.

Chapter Fifteen
[7] 'PSNI - The Police Service of Northern Ireland.
Dander – A familiar Irish word that means a leisurely walk at ease. It seems to be used chiefly in the North of Ireland.